WHITE/BLACK RACE MIXING

WHITE/BLACK RACE MIXING

An Essay on the Stereotypes and Realities
of Interracial Marriage

by

LeRoy Gardner

PARAGON HOUSE
St. Paul, Minnesota

Published in the United States of America by

Paragon House
2700 University Avenue West
St. Paul, Minnesota 55114

Library of Congress Catalog-in-Publication Data

Gardner, LeRoy, 1924-
    White/black race mixing: an essay on the stereotypes and realities of interracial
marriage / by LeRoy Gardner.
       p. cm.
    ISBN 1-55778-796-4
       1. Miscegenation–United States. 2. Interracial marriage–United States. 3. Sex
customs–United States. 4. Afro-American men–Social conditions. 5. Racially mixed
people–United States. 6. United States–Race relations. I. Title.

E185.62 .G37 2000
306.84'6–dc21

                                     00-034659

10 9 8 7 6 5 4 3 2 1

For current information about all releases from Paragon House,
visit the web site at http://www.paragonhouse.com

DEDICATED TO TRUTH

And ye shall know the truth,
and the truth shall make you free.

—St. John 8:32

I have a dream that one day this nation will rise up and live out the true meaning of its creed—"We hold these truths to be self evident, that all men are created equal."

...I have a dream that my four little children will one day live in a nation where they will not be judged by the color of their skin but by the content of their character...where little black boys and black girls will be able to join hands with little white boys and white girls and walk together as sisters and brothers.

—Martin Luther King, Jr., August 28, 1963

CONTENTS

CHAPTER 1
White/Black Race Mixing

AMERICA, "The land of the free and home of the brave," is allegedly a haven for the oppressed and downtrodden. Immigrants from virtually every continent and nation still come to these shores seeking freedom and opportunity, with the exception of black Africans, who were ripped from their motherland, chained and shackled, and cast on foreign strand. Shorn of humanity born; stripped of freedom, naked, hopeless, and forlorn.

This nation is indeed a "melting pot," a cauldron of race mixing. Europeans have practiced sexual activity with the native Indian population since their arrival—however, this treatise is not about such activity.

During slavery, escaped slaves would often be taken in by Indian tribes, which is certainly understandable; the two oppressed nonwhite people had much in common. Many of these male slaves were physically big and strong, dominant in persona, and became warriors and rose to leadership. Needless to say, romantic/sexual relationships developed. Interestingly, my mother's father, "Big Papa" Washington, an emancipated slave, married an Indian maiden in Oklahoma. This union produced three offspring including my mother, Lena.

Mixed-race Lena married Littleton Gardner, the progeny of a mixed-race mother who was the progeny of the slave master and one of his female chattels. To this union, I and four other siblings were born. Note this scenario: I and my dear sister and three brothers (now deceased) have European, Indian, and African ancestry. I'm mixed-race but I've always considered myself an African American. I am in reality a product of the "melting pot" syndrome; truly American. Because of the specter of pervasive racism, my psyche has been conditioned by the nomenclatures of colored, Negro, black (and my skin color is not black), and now African-American to ever be separate, suspect, unequal, denied, and excluded. America, America, may God not forgive, for you know what you do....

From the day the first slaves arrived on these shores, some white males, who of course exercised undisputed power, took sexual advantage of female chattels. During this dark era in American history, sexual activity between white males and female slaves, though never attaining respectability or social acceptance, was not actively condemned. It was common practice for the slave master to select young, healthy female slaves for his exclusive sexual pleasure. These females lived in enforced concubinage, sometimes receiving better housing, clothing, food, and perhaps privileges not afforded the other slaves. On some plantations such females were sometimes quartered in the master-house, trained in the culture and etiquette of the day and available for the comfort and pleasure of male guests.

Adolescent sons of slave owners were often permitted to select a black "wench" who represented an acceptable sexual outlet and prevented promiscuity with the daughters of neighboring plantation owners. Impregnation of the "wench" was encouraged since this insured a constant supply of "mulatto" children, who were in great demand as household servants, bringing double the price of pure black slaves. No effort was made to curtail the violation of black womanhood; every effort was made to protect the "purity" of white womanhood.

After emancipation, the philandering southern male did not miraculously lose his desire for his black paramour. Sometimes he became emotionally impacted. No longer is she his black female chattel; now he has to curry her favor. What a deserved dilemma! Under cover of darkness, sex-seeking white males regularly visit black neighborhoods seeking "nice, clean colored girls." Tragically, many young females are introduced to prostitution by greedy, mercenary sex-procurers or pimps.

Are you wondering why white males from laborer to professional, from pauper to wealthy scion, seek black sex partners? Are you wondering why an intelligent, successful, productive white male married to a beautiful, charming, cultured Anglo-Saxon female would seek a nocturnal rendezvous under the most sordid circumstances, in a most unromantic atmosphere in the ghetto with a black, possibly AIDS infected prostitute? Why would he jeopardize his marriage, career, reputation, even his life and limb to have sex with a black harlot?

I don't know all the answers, however psychologists are agreed. Promiscuous sexual activities, whether premarital or extramarital, may be symptomatic of deep-seated emotional or psychological problems. Perhaps the following considerations will shed some light on the subject.

First, let us consider the "love goddess" image versus the "sex symbol" that grew out of the concept in Western society that true love does not include the erotic. A very definite line is drawn between "love" and "sex," and far too many men are unable to reconcile or merge the two. One loves and marries the "love goddess," and indulges in sex with the other. Psychologists, marriage counselors, and ministers alike recognize that love and sex must be merged in a satisfactory marriage relationship. Men who fail to merge the two are self-conscious and embarrassed, and such men can even be rendered impotent while engaging in sexual intimacies with a "love goddess." In order for him to function effectively in the sex act, he must have a "sex symbol" partner. This type of female represents the "bad" girl and merits no love or respect. In a relationship with this type of female, the elements of tenderness or affection, desires and needs, no matter how inordinate or aberrant, including cunnilingus and fellatio.

The black female is the perfect "sex symbol" to many white males. Such a male considers her his social inferior, perhaps even barbaric, exotic, erotic, sexually uninhibited, an ideal sex partner. He can express sexual inclinations and perform acts with her that he would be ashamed to reveal to his beautiful "love goddess" wife.

Secondly, let us consider the emotional vacuum that exists in many American marriages, which can be due to numerous factors. American white males are often reluctant, less poised, and perhaps less vocal in discussing their sexual attitudes and desires to their wives than, for instance to southern Europeans, Latin Americans, African-Americans and other supposedly less sophisticated groups. Perhaps civilization, with all its attendant complexities and implications and nuances, is responsible for these developments. However, it seems, some white males cannot and do not effectively concentrate on necessary emotional communication with their partners during lovemaking. This lack of emotional communication with their partners causes a rift, seriously affecting, if not destroying, compatibility between the partners. Silence in the bedroom is deadly to mutual satisfaction.

Resentment, anger, fear, or worry on the part of either party can be a major obstacle to sexual compatibility. A great many of the sexual difficulties in marriage may not necessarily be due to ignorance, or faulty or even poor technique, which can be corrected, but to repressed anger and frustration on the part of the husband or wife. Many cases of impotence or frigidity can be traced to an unconscious desire for punishment or revenge against an incompatible or uncooperative spouse.

Often business pressure is the culprit responsible for the emotional vacuum. A harried, ulcer-suffering businessman or executive, worried about production, personnel problems, cost analysis sheets, financial balances, and so on, is in no physical, mental, or emotional condition to "make love" to his spouse at the end of the day. If this situation continues any length of time, the wife will eventually become resentful, unresponsive and emotionally divorced. A vicious cycle develops. The wife rejects the husband, which only adds to his frustration and possible impotence. In such situations some males seek extramarital relationships in an effort to regain their potency, which can and often does involve black prostitutes. A black prostitute is in no position to demand anything other than her price, so is, hence, submissive and cooperative. Her customer's anxieties and frustrations are relieved, so in many cases his sexual potency is restored.

Finally, although the majority of relationships between white males and black females are clandestine, we recognize that occasionally, a white male may become involved in a legitimate relationship with a black female. The reason for this, I believe, lies in the realm of prerogative and choice and does not necessarily relate to any sociological theories or laws of race mixing such as advanced by the late Lester F. Ward, the alleged father of American sociology. Ward's four laws, presented about sixty-five years ago, were based upon the southern concept of white supremacy and consequently received wide and popular acceptance. At this point, it should be of interest to examine these four laws of race mixing as he presented them:

1. The women of any race will freely accept the men of a race which they regard as higher than their own.

2. The women of any race will vehemently reject the men of a race which they regard as lower than their own.

3. The men of any race will greatly prefer the women of a race which they regard as higher than their own.

4. The men of any race, in default of women of a higher race, will be content with women of a lower race.

I now translate the fourth law: "White men in default of white women, will be content with black women." Certainly, this law may be operable in isolated situations under adverse or uncontrollable circumstances or opportunistic situations. For instance, a white man cast upon a tropical island inhabited by primitives may choose a native female and may be temporarily content. However, in the Americas, no white man needs to be content with a black woman in default of white women, for white women greatly outnumber black women. However, we must recognize that there are some white men who prefer and choose black women over white women. And certainly the vast majority of black men prefer black women who, allegedly, represent a lower race. So, Ward's law falls under analytic scrutiny and must be relegated to the realm of personal opinion, which invariably is of value only to the one holding such opinion.

We must therefore conclude that white men or black men or men of any race will be attracted to and prefer the women of any race, including black women, for varied and valid reasons that are operable in the heterosexual relationship.

However, the white male-black female association, which usually is clandestine and promiscuous, seldom resulting in marriage, is not the serious contention. The contention is the relationship involving the black male and the white female. In the fuzzy thinking of most white Americans, black male/white female race-mixing invariably involves a contumacious black male and pitiably disturbed white female. This situation is understandably irritating to most whites who may react emotionally and perhaps unreasonably if a daughter or someone dear is involved—perhaps even hysterically and in many cases violently.

CHAPTER 2
The Issue

In past generations (1930s through 1960s), the strongest barriers to the social acceptance of white/black intermarriage were the antimiscegenation laws in 26 states such as Alabama, Arkansas, Delaware, Florida, Maryland, Mississippi, Missouri, Oklahoma, Louisiana, Indiana, Kentucky, North and South Carolina, Georgia, Texas, Tennessee, West Virginia, and Wyoming. Many citizens now residing in these states are unaware of the sordid history of race relations in them. Thankfully these laws have been declared unconstitutional and removed from the books. However, they are still bastions of racism. There is still widespread opposition to white/black interracial relationships and on interracial marriage.

Many serious issues in the area of race relations face America today:

1. Efforts to dismantle Affirmative Action. In the state of California, white voters overwhelmingly voted for Proposition 209, outlawing Affirmative Action,which Judge Thelton E. Henderson granted a preliminary injunction. The concern of most black Americans is that this legislation

will be the vanguard for other states following suit.

2. The existence of the "glass ceiling" for black employees in the workplace.

3. The curtailment of school integration and busing of minority students.

4. Housing which involves "white flight" from the inner cities to the suburbs. White persons leaving the cities, which borders on "de facto segregation," has become a concern for many African-Americans.

At the opening of the twenty-first century, there is still strong opposition to white/black interracial marriage. Ironically, with the rise of the concept of "black ethnocentricity," we note increasing opposition among many African-Americans.

The strongest opposition comes from adherents to the myth of "white supremacy," who fear the legitimization of blacks joining the white race. White racist Roy H. advises us to study the history of Egypt, India, Turkey, and Southern Europe under Moorish rule (700 A.D.-1490 A.D.) during which he alleges that widespread race mixing virtually destroyed the purity of the white race. Within this context, millions of Americans are disturbed by the rise of proponents of "white power" and the neo-Nazis, the skinheads, and other white racist groups who advocate the violent overthrow of the government and the establishment of an America for whites only. The white supremacists argue that the African/Negro is biologically/genetically inferior, and hence should be sent back to Africa. They have no effectual or legal agenda for ridding America of millions of nonwhite citizens short of revolutionary genocide, which the Nazis failed to accomplish during the Holocaust against the Jews in World War II. May we never forget this horror, which lives in the annals of infamy, and always make sure that no such atrocity will never happen in America.

Thirty years ago such a position was supported by men such as R. Ruggles Gates, then one of the world's leading human geneticists; psychologist Henry E. Garrett, professor emeritus, Columbia University; Dr. Robert Gayre, former professor of anthropology of the University of Saugor, India; and zoologist/author Wesley C. George, professor of anatomy at the University of North Carolina.

These professional scientists agreed and firmly believed that there are vast differences within the human family, not only in physical appearance but in such matters as adaptability to varying environments and in deep psychological and emotional qualities as well as in mental ability and capacity for development. Further, they were of the opinion that nothing was to be drawn from the biological sciences to support the view that all races and types of homo sapiens or various ethnic groups are alike, or will become so in the foreseeable future.

In additional support of such theories, the supremacists cite the prevailing primitiveness of the black man in Africa. They remind us that no purely black culture has ever approximated the high degree of civilization produced by European and Western cultures.

They adduce that interbreeding with the black man is the underlying cause of the low standard of living, the cruel poverty, the lack of scientific achievement, and lawlessness in Latin American countries. They therefore conclude that interbreeding with blacks would have a deleterious effect upon the racial purity of white America, resulting in disastrous social, political, and economic consequences.

Many individuals who firmly believe that interracial mixing is morally wrong glibly quote in the Bible support. The fact is, the Holy Writ is decidedly mute on the subject of Gentile race mixing or intermarriage. There are, however, Biblical statutes and laws prohibiting Jew and Gentile intermarriage, which is of religious significance only. This is another example of how prejudice attempts to speak with theological or scientific authority on subjects of which it knows very little and in some cases nothing.

Some of these same individuals who are so vocally opposed to interracial relations in the daylight, silently condone such activity as long as it is done in the "black ghetto" under cover of darkness. I have personally been approached by white males on occasions seeking a "nice, clean Colored girl."

Their inconsistent equation is this: miscegenation, or illicit sexual intercourse, between white males and black females that results in a mixed race progeny upgrades the black race to a higher intellectual capacity and responsiveness to Western culture, and hence is permissible. On the other hand, black male and white female sexual activity can only result in a progeny of lesser intellectual capability. This practice is the epitome of hypocrisy.

In support of the first part of their equation they refer to some mixed bloods, such as Booker T. Washington, an educational icon who established the historic Tuskegee Institute during the Reconstruction era after the Civil War; militant abolitionist Frederick Douglas, sociologist/author Dr. W. E. B. Dubois; renowned author James Weldon Johnson; charismatic congressman/minister/pastor/author Reverend Adam Clayton Powell; scientist/physician Dr. Charles Drew, who isolated blood plasma; Caucasian-appearing Walter White, former president of the NAACP; and Dr. Ralph Bunche, outstanding geopolitical statesman. However, they can present no valid evidence that their race mixing was the result of sexual activity between a white male and a black female.

The late Carlton Putnam of the *Putnam Letters* fame,

an avowed and vocal "white supremacist," was a more competent writer than logician. Writing in his controversial *Race and Reason,* he argues, "If the production of children is a major objective in legalized intermarriage, the social consequences would be quite different." When intermarriage is permitted on a large scale, the trend is toward a gradual change in social attitudes of acceptance, with a consequent changing of the moral standards of society. On the other hand, the resultant offspring of illicit unions between the two races who are considered "black" are isolated by legal or paralegal segregation; they are given no opportunity to change the moral standards of white society. This then is the philosophical basis for the legal segregation which thankfully no longer exists. However, the philosophy has not entirely disappeared.

One needs no degree in biology or anthropology to understand that the interbreeding of the estimated 12 percent African-American ration with the almost 90 percent white ration in America can in time result in the eventual complete absorption of the black population. In fact, it takes only three to four generations to complete this development. The black population being in the minority and operating in a sphere of low influence would have positively no comparable chance of changing the standards of the dominant white society. As the Reverend G. W. Walker, former publisher of the *National Christian* clarifies: "The broad way to a lost race is for the black man to amalgamate with the white race." However, the white racists don't equate it so. They see only a white race being mongrelized and eventually being destroyed by the infusion of black blood.

And so, the white racists decrees, the only effective preventative is rigid segregation. The celebrated Swedish sociologist Gunner Myrdal in his *American Dilemma,* lists the white racist argument against race mixing in the following order:

1. Intermarriage;

2. Social integration;

3. Integrated facilities, schools, churches, restaurants, parks, etc.;

4. Political enfranchisement;

5. Equal job opportunities and housing.

The order of this listing is a distortion of truth, for the black American's goals are precisely reverse, with the exclusion of inter-marriage, which is definitely not one of our goals in our fight for civil liberty.

Six sociologists interviewed by *U.S. News and World Report* agreed that African-Americans are far less interested in marrying whites than most whites seem to think.

On the other hand, there are more liberal whites who condemn rigid segregation but yet are gravely concerned about inter-race relations. Many of them believe that if black Americans are given educational equity, it will be difficult to deny them vocational employment opportunities with higher attendant wages. With increasing economic and financial stability, it will be impossible to prevent him from purchasing a home where he chooses and can afford. This can bring the problem next door. If he moves next door, there may certainly be a possibility that his son may perchance become interested in one's daughter or vice versa. God forbid.

A northern sociologist evaluates it thusly, "Fair housing practices results in school integration, followed by social integration which is the prelude to interbreeding."

It is impossible to keep white and black children apart after school when they have been involved in integrated school activities during the day.

We note a consequent pattern of conjecture, distortions, irrationality, stereotype conceptions, untruths, race prejudice, and discriminations evolving among not only segregationist but among liberals as deterrents to race mixing.

CHAPTER 3

Stereotyping and Race Prejudice

Part 1: Stereotyping

The black man has long been the victim of definite stereotypes arbitrarily conceived and accepted by much of white society. The word "stereotype" is a term expressing mental attitudes or conceptions whereby people are classified not according to facts but as a result of personal opinions. Therefore, a stereotype is a conception originating in assumptions rather than in conclusive facts. It is an attribution of the virtues or vices of one member of a group to all members. Or it is the prejudging of one person by ascribing to him the good or bad characteristics which are assumed to be universally true of all members of the group of which he is a member. Or it is the evaluation of all members of the group by the observable characteristics or behavior of one. For instance, one black person steals, hence all are thieves; a group of blacks engage in acts of violence, therefore each individual black person is adjudged vicious and potentially dangerous.

In the thinking of a large segment of white society, the black man is conceived of as a clown, buffoon, docile in character, spineless, and overly superstitious or debauched, criminal and is inclined to violence and murder. Such notions have been perpetuated by considering him as an obsequious simpleton in literature; by casting him in servile and menial roles in motion pictures and television sitcoms, and by magnifying his crimes in the news media. A white criminal is given a third-page bottom-of-the-column coverage, while a black criminal rates first-page coverage with a picture.

Generally speaking, stereotypes are sincerely believed and propagated by white society. Numerous individuals pride themselves in presuming to know the black man better than we know ourselves. Some, in fact, consider themselves to be more or less authorities, claiming to know not only what we think but what we want and desire in life. Further, they take great pride in predicting black persons' behavior under certain prescribed conditions.

All stereotyping is not derogatory, but nevertheless it denies a person's individuality and basic human dignity. In some instances it takes the form of faint praise while masking underlying contempt and disrespect. Some praise the black person in voice yet damn him by denying him the admirable qualities of intelligence, strength of character, ambition, assiduity, or nobility of purpose. For instance, they might say that the person is a strong, superior worker, sometimes capable of doing the work of two or three ordinary men. Blacks make loyal and faithful servants and will guard with their

life large sums of money entrusted to their care (however, they can't be trusted around trifling sums and
valueless trinkets). How absurd. Black women have a
natural affection for animals and children and delight
in lavishing care on the sick and invalid. Because of
this trait they make excellent nurses and governesses
(but are irresponsible and addicted to lying and stealing). Blacks are more sympathetic than whites and will
not hesitate to give their last dime to a beggar on the
street. And then steal to satisfy their own hunger.

Georgian John S. asserted to me: "Niggers have
good hearts. Better than most white folks and they don't
expect pay every time they do something for you, either." Perhaps that delusion is why we are underpaid,
overworked, and unappreciated. In response to my in-
quiry as to any possible superior qualities possessed by
Black folk he replied, "Of course, it's common knowledge that you people have an inborn sense of rhythm
and are superior singers and dancers and can run like
gazelles." I didn't want to deflate his flawed ego, so I
refrained from informing him that I couldn't carry a tune
in a bucket. I wanted to add that all black persons aren't
Nat King Cole or Lou Rawls or Luther Vandross, and
certainly all black females aren't Patti LaBelles or
Whitney Houstons.

He continued, "You people excel over white athletes because you are just a few generations from the
jungle. Genetically, you people have longer legs and

stronger Achilles tendons, which equip you to outrun lions and tigers." Note the subterfuge of this form of stereotyping; flattery combined with insult.

I now introduce a more vicious and deleterious form that is an obvious and contrived attempt to degrade, debase, and discredit the black man. It is a calculated, effective expression of the white superiority ethic designed to justify the ill treatment, exploitation, and exclusion of black people. Following are some of the pet stereotypes in this derogatory vein: "The black man is mentally inferior, has limited intellectual powers of concentration which handicap him in scientific and technical fields and is therefore incapable of ever achieving higher educational goals," harangued suburbanite Roscoe H....

In hindsight, I'm sorry that I failed to mention some of the outstanding scientists and inventors of African ancestry such as Joseph V. Nichols and Lewis H. Latimer (incandescent light bulb, which Thomas Edison got the credit for in 1881); Andrew J. Beard, rotary engine, 1892; George W. Kelley, steam table, 1897; the typewriter, Lee S. Burridge and Newman R. Mashman; printing press, 1878, W. A. Lavalette, and numerous others whose inventions greatly improved the quality of life the world over. History could not ignore the contribution of Dr. George Washington Carver, who developed over three hundred products from the lowly peanut. Garrett A. Morgan invented the first traffic light in 1923 and was one of the few Black inventors who profited monetarily when General Electric paid him over forty thousand dollars, a sizable fortune back then. I personally met Frederick Jones, who invented the air conditioning unit for trucks for Northrup King Company in 1949. Regrettably, the misperception that black persons were not inventors still persists. Not all inventors were male. Female doctor Patricia Bath, a professor at Howard University, and a highly accredited ophthalmologist, invented the Laserphaco probe, a revolutionary laser technology for removing cataracts in 1988. I'm personally grateful to her because I received this treatment on both of my eyes in 1995. Since receiving a U.S. patent in 1988, she has received patents in Canada, Europe, and Japan.

Very few African-Americans have gainfully capitalized from their inventions, which in far too many cases were stolen from them, the credit for their inventions going to whites. The inventors listed here is a mere scratching of the surface. Patent examiner Patrick Sluby of the U.S. Patent and Trademark Office in Washington, D.C., has authored a book listing close to a hundred black inventors entitled *Creativity and Inventions*. I'm of the opinion that it should required be reading in public schools all over the nation. Another malicious stereotype is that the black male is incapable of controlling the baser impulses, is oversexed and has a voracious and inordinate passion for white women, no matter how old and unattractive they might be. I find this stereotype to be the most cruel, rendering its victim indefensible and suspect. Other stereotypes place the black man's character in question and alter his position and status, but this one places his very life in jeopardy. Literally, thousands of innocent persons have been brutalized and lynched because an incensed mob exploded with violence when goaded by the very thought of a black man with a white woman. I'm so pleased that the book *To Kill A Mockingbird* was produced as a motion picture starring Gegory Peck.

Thus, we see that stereotyping emerges as a rationalization, an escape from reality, and a justification for the race superiority ethic and reprehensible race prejudice and violence.

Part II: Race Prejudice

Every phase of black life in the United States is touched or even permeated by some form of racial prejudice and is therefore significantly related to the inter-race/male-female association complex. An analysis of the various theological or sociological theories on prejudice, such as the "primary sin," the "vicious circle," the "frustration-aggression," or the "self-centeredness," would not appreciably aid this treatise, therefore, we will confine our analysis to that aspect of prejudice which relates specifically to the subject of white/black associations.

Webster's Dictionary defines prejudice as a "preconceived judgment or opinion; unreasonable predilection: especially an opinion or leaning adverse to anything without just grounds or before sufficient knowledge." Race prejudice consists therefore of preconceived opinions or attitudes that are not based upon actual facts relating to or concerning a particular race.

Individuals who practice race prejudice tend to stereotype the members of the race toward which they direct their bias. This type of categorizing is neither intelligent nor rational and without doubt works toward the disadvantage of the individuals who are the hapless victims of such prejudice.

The prejudiced person must justify his or her attitude and position, so they will endeavor to make their position appear both logical and right. For example, prejudiced whites will attempt to justify their prejudice on the grounds that all black persons are dirty, ill-smelling, ignorant, brutish, immoral, and so on, hence it isn't immoral or wrong to discriminate against them, segregate them, or even despise them or hate them.

However, since race prejudice cannot be justified from a rational or scientific standpoint, they then resort to rationalizations. For example, blacks are intellectually inferior and irresponsible to higher educational standards, therefore it is folly to attempt to educate them. As African-Americans acquired education and proved that we could Indeed respond to the requirements of higher education, it was theorized that such endeavors frustrated and made us unhappy. As many of us achieved success in the professions, in scientific and related fields and business, it was further rationalized such successes with their resultant financial rewards only exposed us to wants and desires foreign to our primitive nature, which further compounded our frustrations. I was told this by a prejudiced employer in his attempt to dissuade my audacious request for a raise in salary.

"What do you need a raise for? You people don't know what to do with money anyway. You don't need as much money as we do. You can live on cornbread and beans and fat-back."

I desperately needed the job, but I quit immediately to keep from slapping him in the face. Interestingly, he couldn't understand my anger. That was an example of how prejudice blinds one to reality.

Many who are blinded by race prejudice are firmly convinced that the black man is the "missing link," that elusive but vital link between the anthropoid ape and primordial man, hence it is extreme folly not to segregate him. This fantastic concept is entirely without scientific credence. In fact, scientific research has established and the American Medical Association has confirmed that all human blood is classified by type and not by race. The blood of different races is compatible and tolerable in any person who has the same blood type. In addition, the human system will not tolerate the blood of animals nor animals the blood of humans. Attempts at crossbreeding animals of different species have been unsuccessful, whereas different races of men readily intermix. Experiments in crossbreeding different animals from the same family tree produce a hybrid, such as the horse with the donkey producing a mule. However, the hybrid is usually sterile.

The question is now posed: How and when did a crossbreeding take place between a simian and a humanoid begetting a black man? And if the black man is a hybrid, he defies theory because without contradiction he is far from sterile and has irrefutably established himself as a most prolific breeder.

Race prejudice is not instinctive nor inherent but rather acquired. Children in their naivete regard superficial differences in facial features, hair texture, the lack or presence of skin pigmentation as incident and accept or reject a person merely upon likes or dislikes. White children play with and accept black children readily without analyzing differences. The black child will be simply regarded as "good or bad" just as the white child will be regarded by the black child.

A white mother and child got on a bus in which I was riding. As they approached me, the child exclaimed, "Mommy, look! That man's face is dirty!" The mother grabbed the child's arm and attempted to drag him to a seat, saying nothing.

The mother verbally attacked the child. "You shut

up your dirty little mouth. Don't say another word!" and pulled him into the seat next to her. Reliable psychologists and social scientists refute the assertion that race prejudice is innate in human nature. The conclusive and incontrovertible fact is, prejudice is a learned reaction, and the social system provides the soil and climate for its germination, growth, and propagation. Here in America, the black man has been stripped of dignity, respectability, decency, yea, even humanity and is thus established by the social setting as an approved, legitimate, and ideal object upon which the feeling of prejudice and can be vented.

Prejudice therefore appears as the result of attitudes, emotional responses, and verbal expressions on the part of parents, teachers, friends, playmates, and in some cases, even clergymen.

I had occasion to overhear a white child remark to another, "I can't play with Johnnie anymore because he's a nigger." I asked who told him that Johnnie was a nigger. "My Daddy and he knows," he replied, and added, "All niggers are bad and will cut off your head with a knife." And sadly, his father was pastor of the church.

Here is a personal experience that illustrates the point. We purchased a house in an area where only a few black families were living. Our children were little and readily accepted by the children living next door. I seldom returned from work until late in the evening, therefore the parents didn't discover my racial identity until Sunday, which caused them extreme concern. They immediately forbade their children from playing with our children. Later that afternoon, despite the ban, one of their children came over to play with our daughter, Sharon, who was about five or six years of age.

I heard some commotion out in the yard and went to the door. I heard the father harangue as he dragged the protesting child home, "Don't you ever let me catch you playing with that nigger again!"

"But she's nice and I like her," objected the youngster.

"I don't care. She's still a nigger and I don't want you associating with her nigger brother," retorted the enraged father as he emphasized his point by soundly thrashing the defenseless tot.

My sympathy went out to the poor innocent being victimized and brutalized by a prejudiced father. The physical pain would subside but the mental scars from the lash of prejudice would remain.

The thought patterns and attitudes of the white child are influenced and molded by the cultural factors and mores in race in his environment. In the South they are still treated as such. They soon learn that black persons are not welcomed at the school or church that they attend, are prohibited from attending their social function, and above all must be kept from association with white women except in a servile capacity. At an early age, they discover that there are unwritten laws for white folk and others strictly for black folk. Whites have much liberty under the law; blacks have very little and in some area none. Whites are first-class citizens, enjoying the privilege of legal recourse and can demand justice; black persons are second-class citizens, if citizens at all, and have few civil or legal liberties and are discouraged from demanding any.

Racism in America is based on the theory of the alleged God decree of the "Divine Right" of white supremacy. All other racial groups have an alleged badge of inferiority which subjects them to the control of the white power group. Every "in" group has a corresponding "out" group that personifies all that is considered repulsive and despicable and thereby justifies the former's ill-treatment, exploitation, and even extermination. The Italian Fascists had their barbaric Ethiopians, who were decimated under the psychopathy of Benito Mussolini; madman Adolph Hitler's Nazi regime had their "Juden Schwein"; the Spanish conquistadors had their "savage natives"; the European settlers in North America had their "uncivilized, murderous Indians"; the American "white supremists" have their "diseased, parasitic niggers." It is soon instilled in the white child's mind that his is the "superior" place; the black man's is the "inferior," and whatever treatment he affords the black man is therefore justified and in no way related to morality or right. In fact, prejudice declares, whatever the "superior" does is right.

Prejudice in its extreme is virulent and destructive, blinding its adherents to facts, truths, and actualities. It rides into town on the tail of half-truths and lies, gets invited and welcomed into the most elite circles, spreads its poison like an epidemic, leaving in its wake a plague of suspicion, dissension, hatred, and sometimes violence. In its ultimate reduction it is such a potent emotional factor it oftimes causes its practitioner to desire the extermination of its object.

Two young black hoboes jumped off a freight train as it slowed into a small southern country town. As they walked toward the center of town, an extremely agitated townsman ran toward them shouting, "There they are! Get those niggers!" Naturally, the two started running....

In short order a crowd gathered and joined in the chase, some out of curiosity, others spurred on by the contagion of the mob. The two frightened, confused hoboes were caught, viciously beaten, dragged through the streets, and brutally lynched, left broken and bleeding, hanging in the public square.

The occasion for such barbarity was the discovery the day before of the badly decomposed body of a young white girl. She had been missing for over two weeks and according to the coroner's report had been dead for at least that period of time. A few weeks later the real murderer, a white criminal, was caught and confessed. The instigator of this horrible lynching was asked why he pointed out the two victims. He hysterically replied, "By God, all niggers are rapist and murderers. They had to be guilty!"

And so prejudice indicts the black man. It decrees without rational investigation or analysis without factual evidence that the black man is subhuman, animalistic, stupid, criminal, violent, and rapacious. It arbitrarily declares that all black males lust after white women, and that their highest ambition is to get involved with one. Prejudice has been the black man's arresting officer, jailer, jury, judge, and often his executioner.

The indictment still stands; the black man has been accused of desiring above all else to intermarry with whites. He has been refused a just hearing and, contrary to the essence of the law, which is justice, has been denied due process of law and declared guilty before trial.

Shall we in an effort to be fair—not, I remind you, to be merciful for oftimes mercy presumes guilt, but simply to be just—give the black man an opportunity to answer these charges?

Do whites really represent the ideal romantic image to blacks? Do black males have an inordinate desire for white females? What exactly are the black man's goals, ambitions, and aspirations in relation to interracial relationships or inter-marriage? Recognizing that a negligible number of blacks do intermarry, let us determine why. Let us analyze the black male and factors which influence his thinking, decisions, behavior patterns, and perhaps his destiny in regard to amalgamation.

CHAPTER 4
Profile of the Black Male

From that memorable day when a Dutch ship captain unloaded a cargo of "twenty Black Niggers" at a Virginia port in 1619, through two hundred fifty years of the most appalling slavery and an additional one hundred-odd years of so-called freedom, the black man in America has been subject to the control, caprice, and cruelty of his white oppressors. The pages of the history of the black man's former servitude have been stained and marred by the most incredible suffering, inhumane oppression, and bestial treatment ever afforded humans on American soil. The black man in America has been baptized in an ocean of fear and agony; pain and anguish; sweat, blood, and tears. During his enslavement he was treated as subhuman chattels; worked as draft animals; abused, maltreated, and exploited. He was bred and inbred the same as any domesticated animal in order to breed a strong and durable laboring beast.

Under slave conditions, infant mortality was enormously high; only the strongest survived. Children began laboring in the fields at about seven or eight years of age and were required to produce a prescribed quota.

In the year 1939 an ex-slave in his late eighties reported to me that at six years of age he began laboring in the cotton fields and was required to pick fifty pounds of cotton before sundown. The first day he failed and was administered a frightful and painful flogging, which he never forgot. Children were introduced to the lash at an early age.

Many slaves carried the scars to their graves.

The work of adult slaves was oppressively heavy, and the supervision was strict and tightly controlled under cruel and sometimes sadistic overseers. Some of the overseers worked on a quota or bonus system that encouraged extreme exploitation of the slaves. Under such conditions it was no wonder that slaves who didn't die from disease, illness, or accidents were literally worked to death. The average working life span of a strong adult slave was only fifteen to twenty years.

Living conditions were deplorable. Slaves usually lived in dilapidated farms or log cabins measuring perhaps ten by fourteen feet with dirt floors and a fireplace used for cooking and heating. Each family, which consisted of a male and a female, and whatever children they might have, fathered by various black or white males, was allotted a cabin. Slave conditions and accommodations were never adequate or satisfactory. Window shutters were used to keep out insects in summer and cold in winter. Sanitary facilities inside the cabins were nonexistent; water had to be carried from a well or a nearby creek, and sleeping facilities usually consisted of a vermin-infested cot or straw-filled mattress on the floor.

These chattels subsisted on the most meager food rations, getting sufficient and decent food only in preparation to be sold, as one would fatten a hog in the fall. The slave owner "generously" gave his slaves the hog's entrails, feet, tail, some "fat-back" and for a special treat, the hog's head. This, together with some corn, molasses, and whatever vegetables or greens that could be scrounged from the field, constituted the slave's fare. Of course, this type of food decreased the incidence of dental cavities, which was decidedly advantageous because whatever dental or medical care the slaves received was administered by the local veterinarian with the crudest instruments and skill.

Upon returning to their indescribably filthy cabins, the slaves were often too exhausted to care about cleanliness, so hygiene standards were characteristically low. After an hour or two of desperately needed rest, they would arise and prepare supper, with utensils discarded from the master's kitchen, and eat it voraciously.

Literally thousands died from overwork and untreated physical diseases; pneumonia, tuberculosis, typhoid fever, dysentery, malaria, influenza, and other unidentified diseases. Many simply died of a broken heart. It is amazing that any survived at all, which attests to the unconquerable human spirit.

Slavery on this continent constituted a crime of great

enormity and scope. Thousands died shackled in the holds of slave-ships during the "middle passage." I remind you with heaviness of heart that the Nazi Holocaust lasted about ten years, whereas slavery lasted about two hundred and fifty years. Voiceless and helpless, the number of victims will remain uncountable in the annals of infamy. I point out a very significant aspect of the slave trade; the participation of warring African tribes, who kept slaves themselves and possibly supplied slaves to the slave traders; of African kings and chiefs who readily sold native captives. However, the vast majority of slaves were kidnapped, shipped to foreign lands, and sold.

A Caucasian minister and colleague of mine defensively reminded me, "After all, the African chieftains were just as responsible as the white people." If indeed this were factual, it in no way exonerates the white people, who were supposedly civilized, and for certain the African chieftains had nothing whatever to do with the institution and propagation of such an unchristian and inhumane practice on this continent, which supposedly is the "Land of the Free." I'm not as concerned about the savagery and barbarity practiced by so-called uncivilized heathens among themselves on the "black" continent as I am over the fact that such a horror would be permitted to flourish, supported by civilized society and condoned by the "Christian church" in a land that supposedly is the citadel of freedom and democracy.

The church should hang its head in shame over its complicity as it rationalized, "The suffering of the black man under slavery was more than offset by his fortunate deliverance from a life of idolatry and savagery," says Rev. Andrew J. in defense.

The church *per se* has not yet purged itself of its complicity, even though some church groups have made penitent overtures.

In this context, I'm extremely grateful for the leadership of the Southern Baptist Convention in extending an apology to the African-American community for their complicity in slavery and stance against our thrust for our civil rights during and under the leadership of the late Dr. Martin Luther King, Jr. at their 1996 national convention. May God's richest blessing be upon them.

A well-known argument in the South, which I refuse to accept, was that the slave masters had to treat their slaves with care; feeding, clothing, and housing them well. Strong, healthy males reportedly brought as much as four thousand dollars at the slave auction and were used as breeders or "studs." I reject totally this argument, for it overlooks the foibles of human nature: selfishness, greed, avarice, caprice, anger, hatred, and cruelty which were practiced without compunction on hapless slaves. There was positively nothing good about such a godless system: It was altogether an abysmal horror; full of "putrefying sores," cruel and inhumane to an infinite degree.

It is difficult to evaluate the psychologically and emotionally dysfunctional effects of living under a system designed to break the spirit, stifle initiative, suppress all noble instincts and dehumanize its subjects. Three significant developments in black life here in America emerged as an aftermath of slavery. These are the "demasculinization" of the male, the evolution of a sense of inferiority, and the resultant response of self-contempt and even self hatred.

Demasculinization of the Black Male

The responsibility of the human male is not only to impregnate the female, as is the case among animals, but to love and protect her, to provide for the safety and well-being of their family, and to represent an ideal "father image" to his children. In American society, the black male has seldom been able to function effectively in all these areas. I don't know whether it was by design or as an evolutionary consequence of the slave ethic, but the reality is, the black male has been successfully demasculinized in this society.

In African culture, the male is the undisputed ruler in his household. He provides for his family, protects them from marauding tribes, and jealously guards the virtue of his women, the epitome of masculine strength and courage. The female performs all agricultural tasks such as planting, tilling, and harvesting the crops; preparing, cooking, and serving the meals, and all other household services.

Under the slave ethic, the entire male-female relationship was radically changed. No longer was the black male head of his household: the slave master was. No longer could the female look to her "man" for protection, for he couldn't even protect himself. Under threat of life and limb, he was forced to submit to involuntary servitude, to acquiesce as his children were snatched from his arms and sold; as his women were exploited, violated, and compelled to submit to the passion of the slave master, his sons, or other white males.

Under such conditions, marriage was nonexistent. Most slave couples lived together in a loose-knit, informal relationship.

Whatever, marriage "jumping the broom" ceremonies were performed by a "witch doctor" without benefit of a clergy and had no legal standing. Family ties were of necessity loose and had no recognized status, and the dissolution of a family unit was entirely at the whim and discretion of the slave owner.

Most slave families consisted of a mother whose children were fathered promiscuously by some scarcely known black male or some philandering white male. The vast majority of slave children knew their mother and were subject to being sold as soon as they were two years old, as we were told by our ex-slave grandmother.

Under such conditions the slave male had no opportunity to exercise masculine prerogatives of pursuing and wooing the woman of his choice, marrying her, raising a family, and providing for them.

Another practice which will remain a blight upon the history of slavery and that contributed to the demasculinization of the black male was the "breeding system." Many slave owners maintained a dozen or so robust virile males whose sole activity was to impregnate the young females. During the day they lolled around talking, jesting, vying athletically. They were fed the best food (similar to the "training table" in modern athletics) and required to have sexual intercourse with at least one female each night. Many of these were occasionally rented to neighboring plantation owners as "studs," receiving lavish praise and sometimes gifts of money from their mercenary owners. Such practices could do none else but develop immorality, promiscuity, and sexuality among the slaves. If a man is encouraged or forced to act like an animal, he will respond likewise. On the other hand if he is treated like a man, he will respond as a man.

This sordid tale of disgrace continues as we consider the status of the victimized females under the breeding system.

The most grievous crime that can be committed against a woman is a sex crime. A woman's virtue is her most precious possession; for this to be violated is unforgivable. Defenseless girls became pawns of the system for the exploitation of white and black males alike. The black woman's body was the profit media that fed the avarice of the white slave owner and the vessel of dishonor for the erotic passion of men. Her position was woeful and pitiable to an infinite degree; she could expect no compassion from the white male, could hope for no help and protection from the black. Under such conditions and circumstances she could have no respect from the black male, whose image was further eroded as he became an accessory to the white man's crimes against her.

Every effort was made to thwart the black male's masculine impulses. There were set before him no noble goals to attain; no horizons to conquer. His ambitions to better himself were thwarted and stifled. He was prevented from learning to read but had to speak the language of his oppressor. Whatever plans he devised to escape often died with the specter of severe and oftimes fatal punishment. Many attempted, to their woe; very few succeeded. Those who didn't seldom lived to attempt it again. The bleeding, broken bodies of captured slaves with eyes gouged out, some with severed hands and limbs, served as dramatic and effective deterrents to others with like ambitions.

A slave must have his spirit broken; his will bent as one bends a sapling to make a straight tree. His will had to conform to his master's will; his body had to be his master's tool; his very life, his master's possession. And so the black male could not be permitted to be a "man." No price was too high to pay; no effort too extreme or cruel to prevent it. He must under and in all circumstances be a "boy" until his beard and head became hoary and white, at which time he became "uncle."

In the eyes of his woman the black male was not a stalwart protector, not a bulwark of security; but a black brute driven by unbridled and animalistic passion, consorting with her oppressor; a feared and hated accomplice in her exploitation and violation. He indeed was a male, but for certain he was not a man!

In the eyes of his offspring, he was not a courageous conquering hero; he was a nameless black stranger who caused his mother to cry out and moan in the deep dark night. And then he was gone as quickly and silently as he had come. The child was frightened and confused. Who was he? Why had he come? What had he done to Mommie that caused her to sob and cry for hours after he had left? The child promised himself that when he became of age; he would be A MAN and protect and help his mother.

In the eyes of white society, the black male has never been a man willing and choosing to fight or die rather than be enslaved; he never had the courage to die heroically rather than live ignobly. The black male was nothing more than a spineless, groveling, cowering chattel. The ultimate goal had been reached; the supreme end had been achieved: the black male now stood shorn of his humanity, stripped of his masculinity; naked, indecent, conquered, alone, he was helpless and hopeless.

Evolution of a Sense of Inferiority

Under the slave ethic, the black man was constantly reminded that he was inferior and treated as such. As he emerged from slavery he was confronted with a smoldering resentment, overt discrimination, and segregation on every hand.

From elementary school through high school a definite program was designed to instill a sense of inferiority in black children as preparation for later conformity to the pattern of segregation.

I have vivid recollections of teachers who at the beginning of the school year required their pupils to reveal their racial and or national background. This practice appeared innocent enough on the surface, causing no embarrassment to white children, and would have caused none to the black children if the teacher had refrained from prying and merely accepted an answer of "Negro," which was the accepted term at that time. And even at the threshold of the twenty-first century, I along with many are perfectly comfortable with the term. So within this context, I will use this term. All lighter-hued "Negroes" are products of amalgamation, but in some cases it is nigh unto impossible to determine or identify the various racial mixtures in their makeup, with the exception of a degree of African ancestry. The problem in many cases where white blood exists is that the parental union was probably promiscuous between a white male and a black female or between a black male and a white female.

Now in regard to the "Negro" pupils in question, the reminder of parental illegitimacy or being the off-spring of a promiscuous union invariably was most painful. I have seen sensitive girls so embarrassed and hurt, they would burst into tears and run out of the classroom. One pupil was so disturbed she refused return to the classroom.

The erosion sets in as the black child's paternity is discredited and that of the white child is favorably contrasted. The favored white children appear "pure"; the black children appear illegitimate, "impure" or "mongrel." The white children feel proud; the black, shame!

The deterioration continues as the home life of caucasians and blacks is contrasted. "Negro" pupils were deeply embarrassed as they reported that their fathers (if indeed they were living with them) were shoe-shiners, janitors, barber-shop porters, or hotel doormen while the white pupils presented their fathers as professionals, businessmen, realtors, salesmen, and the like. And certainly the mortification was not lessened as some had to reveal that their family was on welfare or AFDC. There are many questions and statements, though inadvertently asked or uttered, that can contribute to the erosion of a black youngster's personality and are a factor in instilling a sense of inferiority. And the elementary teacher asked her pupils what they wanted to be when they reached adulthood. One black expressed an ambition to be the President of the United States, which brought a malicious retort from the teacher, "That's ridiculous! You must be more realistic. No black man will ever be President of the United States!" And all the white children laughed.

Perhaps she was being realistic and honest in her naivete, but she effectively eroded the black youngster's aspiration. Oftimes accomplishment begins as a childish dream. And dreams oftimes become reality. The fruition of attainment and fulfillment oft begins with a childish dream, yea an acorn of a dream can blossom into an "oak tree" of achievement. In far too many instances, the callousness or downright ignorance of a teacher has caused irreparable psychological damage to the impressionable minds of these youths.

The thought patterns, responses, and motivations that effect children all the rest of their lives are established at the elementary school level. Deep psychological wounds often result from being told that one is inferior intellectually and is unwanted and despised, the offspring of savages and slaves.

The school curriculum offered black students in segregated schools is of a lower standard and designed to prepare them for less skilled and nonprofessional occupations. In some northern schools we were advised against taking college prepatory courses on the assumption that we lacked the mental ability to pass such courses. When aptitude tests revealed that we indeed had that capability, such students were encouraged to take social science courses on the advice that even if they earned degrees in other fields, they could not hope to gain employment. Needless to say, such practices and bad advice stifle initiative and achievement. Far too many students simply give up with a "why try if I can't succeed" attitude and become another dropout statistic. This attitude is very prevalent among far too many African-Americans and is used as an excuse to do nothing worthwhile.

Multiple scores of African-Americans, feeling that success is denied them, succumb to despair, abandon their hopes and dreams, and attempt to escape into the netherworld of alcohol, narcotics, or crime.

The techniques used to instill a sense of inferiority in black persons have been phenomenally successful, for a large number are convinced that they are inferior and feel shame in being what they are. How psychologically devastating it must be to regret your birth, to blame your parents for begetting you, to even curse God and fate for permitting you to live.

Dark-skinned, crinkly-haired, teen-aged George...

scornfully expressed, "My black mother should've been shot for bringing me into this damn world! I'll hate her until I die!" What must it be like to awaken each day to insults, ephitets, rejections? Millions of black Americans who experience feelings of shame and regret at being subjected to continual invectives and insults, ephitets, and rejections gradually develop a conscious or subconscious self-contempt or self-hatred.

Self-Contempt

There is a well-defined phenomenon in minority groups of contempt for the group, its members, its culture, its music, and its social activities, even for oneself in being a member of the group. Group self-contempt as opposed to group self-respect is negative and degrading. Group self-respect identification is a basic factor in most radical groups, of which the Ku Klux Klan and the Black Muslims (Nation of Islam) in America are outstanding examples. The Ku Klux Klan embraces the tenets of white supremacy; white is superior, hence white represents all that is good, moral, decent, respectful, worthwhile enduring. The phenomenal success of the Black Muslims in America lies in the reversal of this premise, and adapting and promoting the black supremacy myth—black is good; white is evil! Black is truth; white is untrue. Black is honorable; white is dishonorable. Black will eventually conquer white for black is the original color, hence is superior and will eventually perservere! Pure nonsense.

The victims of self-contempt reflect, perhaps not consciously, a well-denied, defeatist behavior pattern of ill-ease in the presence of whites coupled with timidity, servility, and kowtowing. The psychological pattern is reflected in an "I'm inferior, worthless, immoral, incapable, and justly so" attitude.

This self-contempt can manifest itself in all the expressions of bias that characterize the prejudice of members of the majority group; blacks referring to each other in uncomplimentary terms such as: "White is right; yellow is mellow; brown, hand around; black, get back!" "Nigger under the hood, no good." In this frame of mind and reference, it can be construed as a conscious desire to escape identification with the contemptible group.

Here is a sobering experience I had at church one afternoon. The child's evangelism teacher had finished her lesson to the children using the "salvation book":

- Page 1 was completely black. She emphasized, "The human heart is BLACK with SIN and sinners can never be admitted into HEAVEN."

- Page 2 was red. "The Lord Jesus Christ died on the Cross for the sins of mankind. HE shed HIS precious BLOOD to cover our Sins. All who accept HIM as personal SAVIOR will be saved and go to HEAVEN."

- Page 3 was white. "All who accept the Lord Jesus, God cleanses their soul from sin and it becomes WHITE as SNOW and they are admitted into HEAVEN."

- Page 4 was gold representing the streets of heaven. The streets of HEAVEN are paved with pure gold and GOD'S children will play and dance along those streets of GOLD."

After the children were dismissed, I checked the sanctuary before locking up and heard sobbing. I discovered a young male about 10 years old lying on a pew sobbing his little heart out. He sat up as I asked him what was the matter.

Wiping away tears with his hands, he blurted out, "I'm black, and the teacher said that black people with black hearts are going to Hell. I don't want to be black, I want to be white. What can I do?"

He was indeed dark-skinned and black-eyed with black "woolly" hair. In fact his lips were dark colored and his gums were not pink but a dark-hued purple. Of course, I knew his parents, who are dark-skinned.

I was able to convince him that he had misunderstood what the teacher said. I explained that the black page did not represent black people and the white page didn't represent white people. Reading some Bible passages, I emphasized that God loves all people and that God loved him. After prayer and a loving hug, I sent him home.

Since childhood, I have rejected racist images of the "good guy," wearing a white hat and riding a white horse. Conversely, the "bad guy" is always in a black hat, dressed in black, and riding a black horse with murder blasting from his smoking guns.

American literature is not guiltless. The white knight riding a white horse, coming to the aid of white beautiful maiden in distress; the evil black knight dressed in black, riding a black horse, intent on mayhem; the black-haired "vampire" draped in a black cape, lusting after fresh blood.

And the news media is just as guilty: the black criminal is given front-page coverage with a picture.

All of the above can have an adverse effect upon the impressionable minds of some black youths. Many such individuals become psychological/emotional advocates of "escaping from their blackness." Some move to neighborhoods and small towns where there are few or no black persons, enroll their children in predominantly "white schools" and join churches attended primarily by caucasians. Some black individuals who possess no striking "Negroid" features go one step further and successfully "pass" as member of another racial group such as Italian, Spanish, Syrian, or Arabic.

Terry…whose father was brown-complexioned and his mother Native American, claimed his mother's tribal heritage and now receives a monthly stipend from a gambling casino in Minnesota.

He expressed to me, "I'd be a fool to claim my 'blackness' and be unemployed and broke. I'm not interested in beating on a tom-tom nor worshiping Manitoba, but I've got some self-respect and a pocketful of money. Makes sense, don't it?"

Some blacks in order to safely play the game, change their names, birth certificates, and Social Security numbers. As they leave the black world each morning and sojourn in the white world until the end of the working day, they must act white, speak "white," never daring to get careless, even to enduring derogatory references to black folk.

Louise…is an interesting example of intellectual "escapism." She is dark-complexioned and rather obese, but facially pretty. She tried desperately to find a light-complexioned male or even a white male to father a child who would not be as dark-skinned as she was. Strangely, she seemed more committed to being a mother than being a wife, as she was of the opinion that a child would fill the void in her. Being unsuccessful in finding an interested light-complexioned male, she, almost in desperation, paid white males on occasion to have sex with her. To her regret, the strategy was unfruitful.

I still have great respect for her as an individual and

am impressed with her academic achievements; she is gainfully employed in the Education Department and highly intelligent, but I'm still uncomfortable with her decision.

The dear precious lady was artificially impregnated with a white male's sperm at a sperm bank. She was overjoyed when she gave birth to a beautiful café au lait complexioned daughter. It is totally her business, but I'm still of the opinion that every child needs Mom and Dad. Further, I'm of the opinion that the sweet, precious little daughter will have a serious problem dealing with black grandparents whom mother would like to escape from, while having no connection with a paternal family. May someone be merciful.

Amalgamated Kenneth…short, stumpy, with olive complexion, curly black hair, and who to the casual observer could be Arabic, lived such a dual existence. Gesturing vigorously with his hands he articulated his observations of white people.

"Knowing little or nothing about us, most white people fear and distrust us. Consequently, they either completely ignore us or, if forced into contact with us, are dishonest with us and themselves. Many claim to be liberal and devoid of prejudice, which is pure denial."

I was amazed at his depth of insight and level-headed articulation. I appreciated him not painting all whites with a wide brush which would have put him in the camp of the prejudiced.

Those who are emotional advocates of "passing" but choose not to for various reasons, express their group self-contempt in less pronounced ways. Many middle-class blacks, especially some who are lighter complexioned, may sometimes comment on the dark skin color or bad behavior traits of lower-class blacks. In fact, many of them adopt some of the same prejudiced and stereotyped conceptions held by prejudiced whites. Some of these persons frequently use the despised term "nigger" in describing some objectionable person of color. Such expressions as "nigger under the hood; no good," describing a poorly qualified mechanic, or "C.P. time," referring to the tardiness of black persons, are frequently used. Yet if these same expressions were used by a white person, they would be construed as prejudice expressions.

The black "stool pigeon" who reports illegal activities that go on in the black community to law enforcement officers is another example of a manifestation of group-self contempt. By exposing and discrediting the foibles of his own people, this type of individual perhaps receives some degree of psychological expiation from the "sin" of being black.

The "Uncle Tom" type reflects a conceding sense of self-contempt as he overplays the role of feigning docility and kowtowing in the presence of whites, all the while searing with rage because of his skin color. I'm not a physician, but such emotional responses may well contribute the high incidence of high blood pressure among blacks.

African-American children very early experience the ways in which prejudice is commonly expressed, being called derogatory "racial" names by whites and even sometimes by blacks, or maybe even by their parents or thoughtless, ignorant, biased, or antagonistic teachers. Norms and mores of the greater community can and often do add to these innocent children's dilemma. Children born into such an atmosphere cannot help but be influenced by it. Psychological studies can and sometimes do develop a sense of inferiority in those as young as four or five years of age.

I recall vividly my distressing introduction to segregation. My mother took me, my two brothers, and our sister on a train visit to her parents' farm in Oklahoma. I was about six years old. One day my Aunt Gertrude took me along on a shopping trip into town. As we boarded a segregated streetcar, I innocently jumped up on the first empty seat I saw. With a stern command to me, and apologies to the white passengers, she delivered a resounding cuff to the side of my head and roughed me to the rear of the streetcar, where the rest of the black passengers were sitting. The white passengers seemed amused and curiously satisfied. While we rode, my aunt gave me my first lesson in white/black relations in the South. She emphasized that white folks always come first; that I must always use "Yes, sir" and "Yes, ma'am" in addressing white persons; and I should never forget "my place," which wasn't made clear to me at that tender age. And I confess, it hasn't been satisfactorily defined to me yet. Needless to say, the next morning my dear mother and her children boarded the next train heading north. To this day I have no desire to visit my birthplace.

Children of color recognize early in life that black Americans occupy an inferior position to white Americans, and at a tender age some may conclude that they are despicable and unwanted. Since these children are influenced by acts of discrimination, they can't help but learn the same patterns of prejudice that white children learn. Also they oftimes unconsciously reject African-American and "Negro" ways and sometimes despise their skin color. This factor accounts for the large number of African-Americans who almost proudly claim other racial strains in their ancestry.

Another factor in the phenomenon of self-contempt arises out of the frustrations that black persons constantly experience in the caste system as it is in America. When one is forced by mores, norms, and even political and police action to act passively, the hatred that normally would be expressed in aggressive or defensive action toward the abusing force is oftimes turned inward. Such individuals, daring not to commit suicide because of traditional fears, a natural or inborn desire to live, and/or perhaps religious teaching, develop a subconscious desire to strike, harm or even exterminate the "image" of self, which may be any black male or female. This helps to explain the brutality of some black males against their black female "romantic" partners and the high number of aggravated assaults, shooting, stabbings, and homicides that take place in the black communities.

Crime as a Retaliatory Action

There is no question that a disproportionate number of crimes are committed by black persons. The high rate of such crimes has been erroneously attributed to an alleged innate criminal tendency. One writer (whom I earlier referred to) contends that blacks are not capable of comprehending moral or civil law as it is defined, and scientists have attributed the high rate of crimes committed by African-Americans to the social disorganization following emancipation, the migration of Southern Blacks to Northern urban cities, and resultant problems.

These problems are enumerated as overcrowding in substandard housing, discrimination in housing, development of ghettos, inequities in employment and wages and chronic unemployment. Confronted on every side with discrimination, prejudice, hunger, and deprivation, many black persons resort to crime.

Crime as it relates to African-Americans appears therefore symptomatic rather than hereditary, and emerges in many instances as a demonstrable retaliatory reaction against suppression and subjugation. The high rate of crime must be correlated with these problems as they exist in America.

One police commissioner had this to say. "Individuals of lower socioeconomic status often live with lower standards, are more unskilled and less employable, hence unresponsive to social assimilation." These individuals invariably are rejected by the community, which in turn generates antisocial behavior patterns. Rejection breeds revolution! These rejects must get even!

Crime in many instances provides the emotional expression, they need. It is often manifested in fighting among themselves, as has been mentioned. Sometimes it is demonstrated in interracial violence, such as the clashes in New York City between blacks and Puerto Ricans or the recent riots in California and other large metropolitan cities.

In the evaluation of criminal acts committed by blacks a definite retaliatory pattern emerges. Oftimes repressed anger just explodes. The attacker lashes out violently on anyone nearby, male or female, white or black. On occasion police officers are attacked and even killed, with dire results. From interviews with blacks convicted of assault, I have discovered that oftimes this pattern involves compulsive psychopathic behavior. The psychologist is baffled, offering no solution other than confinement in an institution.

One fellow stated, "I get a real charge smashing my fist into the face of whitey!"

Another revealed that every time he assaults and robs a white man, he feels that he is getting even. Whatever money he gets he considers as part payment on the debt owed to his ancestors for their many years of enforced slavery. Obviously such actions are evidence of deep emotional or psychological disturbance. Many so disturbed will not stop short of murder.

Sadistic patterns are discoverable and treatable in preadolescence, but too often the symptoms are unrecognized, ignored, or overlooked. In many instances these patterns have a definite correlation with sexuality and are expressed in assaults and rapes on white women.

One, Arthur P….stated that he has no desire to assault colored women, and that by assaulting white women he's getting even with the white world by desecrating the one thing most prized by white America—white womanhood. One Saturday afternoon he went into town to see a movie. On the way home, as he passed a group of white youths congregated in front of a drugstore, one of the girls pointed to him and said, "that nigger is looking at me!"

Whereupon the white males attacked him, and he was prevented from being severely injured only by the timely arrival of a police car. The police dispersed the crowd and detained the black male.

The white youths accused him of starting the trouble.

The black male was put into the squad car, taken to police headquarters, interviewed, given a sound and brutal thrashing, firmly admonished to never mess with white women and released.

He endured a painful, sleepless night at home. The next morning he packed his bag, bade farewell to his mother, and boarded a bus heading north to Chicago, Illinois. He found employment and was seemingly doing well.

One day while shopping in a supermarket he accidentally bumped into a white female shopper. She incensed him with a loud reprimand. He promptly knocked her down, which attracted a male shopper who gave him a fearful beating. The police came and arrested him.

After being released from the hospital, Arthur appeared before a judge who reduced the charge from aggravated assault to simple assault and gave him ninety days in the workhouse. Upon release, his repressed anger surfaced, and his dysfunctional behavior was unleashed in a number of assaults and rapes on white females. He was eventually apprehended, charged, and sentenced to ten years in the penitentiary.

Alonzo W....dark-skinned, poorly educated, and belligerent, was sentenced to ninety days for slapping a white woman at his place of employment for a personal affront. I asked him how he felt after committing such an act. Almost elatedly, he expressed, "Good, real good! It was as though all the fear and frustrations and hatred from all the abuse and cursings I had taken all my life just exploded…and I would do it again! Yeah, I felt real good. I felt that I was getting even with all the honkeys who had done me wrong."

Another example…a black male bought a round-trip ticket to a northern city. As soon as he got off the bus, he confronted the first white man that he saw and without provocation began beating him. He was promptly arrested, convicted, and sentenced to jail. In jail, he heard that I was a champion of the "underdog" and got in touch with me.

I visited him and inquired into his bizarre behavior. For months he had been haunted by a compulsion to beat up a white man. He knew that if he attempted such a thing in the South he wouldn't live to tell of it, so he decided to come north and "get it out of his system." He served ninety days in the workhouse and was released. He evidently didn't get it all out of his system as he committed a number of assaults, finally stabbing a white female to death. He is now confined in a mental institution for the criminally insane.

Tex B.…a solicitor, or "pimp," has five white prostitutes working for him. He was tall, dark, and I mean dark but not handsome; arrogant, overbearing, and intimidating.

Each night he parked outside bars and adult bookstores waiting for customers, or "tricks." He informed me that many white men approached him because he was black and sitting in an expensive car. He doesn't consider himself a criminal but rather a consultant in the "sex" business. "You receive a consultant fee from the john up front and consultant fee from the prostitute; that's legitimate business?"

"Oh, no. They just pay me a percentage of their money. They have to have money to pay their bills and keep themselves clean and disease-free. In fact, my women get a physical each month. Right?"

I didn't concur so I didn't respond with, "Right." However, I was impressed with his strategy.

His rationalization and cavalier concern for the possible consequences of his criminal activities interested me. He is convinced that if he gets "busted" he will hire a top-level criminal lawyer and beat the "rap."

Did he feel that white society owed him anything? Yes. It had robbed him of his manhood, his self-respect, and of the opportunity to pursue a normal life.

What was his opinion of white people as a whole? As a rule they are dishonest, unscrupulous, and hypocritical. He trusted none of them.

I questioned, "If you don't trust white people, what about the white prostitutes in your stable?"

"I don't trust them; I use them."

I let him rant and rave for a moment or two before continuing my interview.

"How do you feel about the white prostitutes in your stable?"

Pointing his finger at me, he reprimanded, "Reverend, don't change the subject. I'm very critical about you black ministers selling out to the white establishment. You don't worship God, you worship the image of a white Jesus…. And you know perfectly well that Jesus wasn't white with straight hair. He was a Jew with swarthy skin and curly hair. You've got a picture of a white Christ hanging on your church's wall and all of you ass-kissing black fools bow down to it. You're no different from me; I scam white johns and you scam those stupid church members."

I had to respond defensively, "Just one minute, your criticism is without merit, because we have no pictures of white Jesus in our church. I worship the true and living God who is SPIRIT. The Bible declares, 'God is SPIRIT and they who worship him must worship Him in Spirit and in Truth.' Further, I resent you accusing me of scamming the precious members of the church that I serve. And for your information, I don't preach about Heaven to impoverished black folks who are on the bottom rung of the economic ladder and have no bootstraps to lift themselves up. I challenge my people to get an education by helping them to get scholarships at the colleges in the area. I help them get jobs and a paycheck. I assist them in getting loans and inspire them to go into legitimate businesses."

Tex responded, "Okay, so you're not like the rest of them. "If I come to hear you preach, do I have to put anything in the offering?"

"Nope.... What a person puts in the offering is between them and God. If you decide to not contribute to the offering, that's your business. I would be pleased if you and some of your 'harem' would attend." I smiled invitingly.

As he reached into his pocket and pulled out a wad of money, he answered, "I'll think about it." He peeled off a hundred-dollar bill and handed it to me. "Put this in the offering for me."

I thanked him for the contribution and then brought him back to my question concerning how he felt about the white prostitutes who worked for him.

By exploiting white prostitutes and gaining his living from white males, he felt he was getting even with white society.

He challenged, "In your next sermon, tell your people that the blue-eyed devils are not going to pay us reparations for the four hundred years of slavery. They paid the Japanese who were put in concentration camps during World War II a lousy twenty thousand apiece, which was peanuts. They've partially paid the Native Americans for the land they stole. And I'm so glad that the Indians are sticking them up at the gambling casinos. I get a real charge when ever I visit a casino and watch the white dogs being ripped off."

"Are you romantically involved with any of your harem members?"

"Of course, that's how I keep them under my control. You're a biblical man…. King Solomon had seven hundred wives and five hundred concubines. Didn't he?

I shook my head in confirmation as he continued.

"Well, I've only got six concubines…. I handle them all." He revealed that he fathered two children by two of them and doted on a son. He hates them because they are white, yet loves them because they are female; inexplicable! Perhaps a highly competent psychiatrist could unravel his confused thinking; he completely baffled me.

Panderer Tex… is representative of an enigmatic breed of African-American male; proud, arrogant, bold, shrewd, avaricious, vindictive, unafraid of the white man.

Many such males who are motivated by neurotic needs and drives and get involved with white females often cause some serious problems in race relations. Some neurotic blacks consider a white female a status symbol, satisfying themselves that by gaining a white female they have in some degree attained a modicum of equality with white society. Others, having suffered exploitation and rejection, feel that an association with a white female in some way restores their "manhood."

Black males not motivated by neurotic needs who become involved with white females represent a small minority of the more sophisticated members of the professional and middle class.

I must emphasize that, contrary to public opinion, the vast majority of black men have no desire to associate with or to marry white women. They, like most males of any ethnic group, prefer to marry within their own group.

The contemporary African-American male is the end result of a transformation that began at the turn of the century, was accelerated during the two world wars and has steadily gained impetus. As numerous African-Americans acquired the customs, thought, and behavior patterns of American culture, the deep layers of their personality have been affected, transforming them into a "new" image. The extent of this transformation has been in direct proportion to their response to educational and vocational opportunities and their participation in other phases of American life.

The contemporary black male realizes that he is not inherently inferior, that the degree of his achievement in life is dependent wholly upon his sacrifice, and that opportunities must not only be taken advantage of but oftimes must be made. He further realizes that his past inadequacies were not due to a basically lower degree of intelligence but to inequities in opportunity and social descrimination. A person can't hope to achieve if he or she is deprived of the opportunity to try.

Hopefully this transformed male is distinguishing himself in the fields of science and technology, medicine, law, literature, business and finance, education, and the arts as well as in the areas of music and athletics, in which he has long excelled. In many instances, whites underestimate this "new Negro" and are embarrassed and baffled as they are confronted by a man of color who presents a profile of courage and hopefulness, culture and intelligence, fastidiousness in appearance, responsibility in duty, competence in performance, and excellence in achievement.

CHAPTER 5
African-American Female Dominance

The African-American female is a significant factor in our analysis of the interracial picture in America. According to the latest census figures there are more African-American females than African-American males. As a result, the competition for a male is extremely keen among African-American females. Three in every five females over eighteen years of age are single and only two will successfully find a mate. Significantly, a disproportionately large number of these females are widowed, and more than eight million are either divorced, separated, or living apart from their husbands or mates. The proportion of unmarried is higher than among white females. Consequently, an African-American female is not only competing with her sisters for eligible males, she is also competing with her white counterparts who are interested or involved in an interracial relationship.

The African-American female has the same basic drives, ambitions, and goals which include finding a suitable mate, as the white female. Therefore, her resentment of any white female who is involved with a black male is certainly understandable or even justified.

Dominance Factor

One of the most significant factors in the African-American female's profile is a traditional and characteristic dominance. This tradition influences virtually every female regardless of ethnicity but is more pronounced in the African-American female. It grew out of slavery, which devalued the African. On the antebellum plantations of the South, the female slaves ruled their cabins, their children who resided with them, and the male slaves in their lives. The ones whose sexual favors were sought and solicited by the slave masters exercised an unyielding power in the slave quarters.

After emancipation these females were in great demand as domestics and household servants. Many of them found employment as cooks in restaurants and hotels, and as laundry or factory workers. Such employment for the female often constituted the only source of income for the household. This factor, coupled with job discrimination, low wages, and unemployment of the black male (along with the high rate of male desertions), made it easy and sometimes necessary for the female to assume the dominating role in the household. She provided most if not all of the income and invariably made the major decisions in the household. The social and economic status of the female and her decisions in the household had profound psychological and emotional overtones peculiar to the black family.

This female dominance factor can appreciably undermine a satisfactory male-female relationship. Some males confuse the sexual and social roles and see their women as pseudo-masculine nonfemale, and authoritarian. The resultant attitude toward their women is a combination of suspicion, hostility, and resentful dependency. Such feelings, being difficult to hide or disguise, contribute to the development of a vicious cycle; the female becomes progressively unresponsive and uncooperative during intimacies, which in turn aggravates the existing hostility and resentment of the male.

Professional marriage counselors note a high degree of sexual antagonism between black males and females. Numerous couples, failing to find satisfaction in these areas and realizing that they are no longer in love, separate and seek other partners.

These factors significantly affect the high rate of separations, divorces, and desertions by males. Live-ins, promiscuous affairs and illicit unions adversely affect the children of such relationships and are of increasing concern. Many females of color discover early in life (perhaps from an experience with an older sexual partner during adolescence or from their mother's example) that one of the greatest powers they possess in controlling men is SEX. These females use their sexual favors as a weapon to secure money, gifts, favors, and other concessions from their mates forcing them to submit to their dominance. In some cases the female is overly demanding, forcing their mates, to return promptly from work, turn their paychecks over to them and cater to their every whim. In many such couples the male eventually becomes fed up with the controlling tactics, is turned-off, and terminates the relationship. The female then seeks to replace him.

In view of the foregoing implications, factors, and practices, it is not surprising that many such victimized black males seek or take advantage of an opportunity to become involved in an interracial association.

The African-American Prostitute

Most black prostitutes find it more profitable to sell their services to white clients, which contributes to the interracial picture in America. Occasionally such unions result in childbirth, complicating the picture and adding to increasing multiracialism in our society. Many of these females harbor disrespect and some a deep hatred for their white clientele. The consensus is resentment of the white man's exploitation of black women, his reluctance and oftimes refusal to be seen with them in public.

I was impressed by the perception of one such who regularly served a client who paid her two hundred dollars a visit. She was dark-complexioned, tall, heavy breasted, hippy, and decidedly not beautiful facially. But I would imagine that her client in the throes of a sexual episode was not remotely interested in facial beauty. Her sexy figure may have been her best selling point.

In her husky voice she analyzed her clientele. "The white man is 'god supreme' in his office, his domain of power, or in his own social circle, but when he comes to me under cover of darkness, using me to release his 'sick' passions and performing acts which would mortify his wife, he becomes something despicable. Sometimes I get so disgusted I could puke. Some of these devils say things to us that they would never say to a white woman; it's as though we have no feelings, as though we're non-human, as though we're dirt."

How could she expect any other treatment under the circumstances, for after all she was a prostitute deserving of no respect. Though her judgments were far too general and perhaps a little harsh, she introduced me to a labyrinthian world I never knew existed.

We note, however, that with the increase in desegregation, integration in the area of primary associations, and dramatic changes in social organization—such as increasing urbanization and population mobility—and the continuing amalgamation of blacks into the mainstream interracial relationships are emerging from the shadows into the sunlight of tolerance, if not acceptance.

CHAPTER 6
Changing Patterns

Here is an excerpt from a letter received by a pastor of a fashionable urban church:

Dear Pastor:

I am a 33-year-old secretary. I own my home, drive a late model car, and have healthy bank account. I'm intelligent and not unattractive. I'm anxious to find a good husband to share my life. My problem is a handsome, eligible junior executive in the firm where I work who is more than professionably amicable toward me. I wonder if it would be inadvisable or indiscreet for me to invite him to church. My plan is to purposely trap him. I'm impatient to wait any longer for him to ask me for a date, but on the other hand, I don't want to appear too aggressive and chase him away....

This motivation is not uncommon for the female of the species who seems to be motivated by a desire to find and if necessary pursue and marry the male of her choice. I daresay, few marriages would take place if women just sat around waiting and hoping for a "knight in shining armor" to appear and rescue them from their spinsterhood. Men in general are unwilling or at least apprehensive about changing their bachelor status and in many cases need a little prodding. There is without doubt a need for a definite evolution of female aggressiveness in this world of changing patterns.

Male-Female Patterns

We note a significant psychological change taking place in American males that makes it more acceptable for…females to be a little more aggressive in relationships. The American male has generally become less dominating, less aggressive, and more compliant than formerly. In industry and business he can no longer be a "loner," he must be a member of the team. The day of the rugged individualist is passé. The male in order to endure and succeed must be a unit in a complex, a cog in the industrial-commercial machine.

This development affects his social attitude in courtship and romantic involvements. He may be reticent in initiating a relationship—perhaps a little unsure of himself during courtship. So, when a female takes the initiative, he may feel that she has overstepped the bounds of propriety. Further, the natural reluctance of men to change their status of bachelorhood requires a fairly positive attitude when approached by an aggressive female.

Here are some interesting facts. Women are accumulating more money and net worth than men. According to one financial expert, "Man accumulates wealth for the woman to enjoy." For we well know that women outlive men by about five to eight years. Increasing numbers of women are moving into higher paying executive and professional ranks. It is not uncommon for such executives to make salaries comparable to men, in the $50,000 to $100,000 per year bracket.

Over half of industrial stocks are owned by women and well over 60 percent of all savings accounts in banks are owned by them. According to a study conducted by Brad M. Barber and Terrance Odean of the University of California, women are more astute investors than men. According to the study, males take far more risks, trade their stocks too often, and opt for the gamble, whereas females are more conservative.

Statistically, females outnumber males in America because more females are born than males, and females live longer than males. In the larger metropolitan cities such as New York, Los Angeles, Chicago, Boston, and Washington D.C., single women outnumber single men sometimes by as much as three to one. Many women live menless lives. Certainly in the face of such odds, no one could criticize a young female for being a little aggressive in pursuing an eligible male in order to gain a husband and family.

Being unsuccessful in their attempts to catch a white

male, they turn their attentions to black males. Of course, they are treading in "taboo" territory. As one realistically expressed it, "I'm not going to be an old maid if I can help it. The guy I'm in love with is not white and he loves me, is a wonderful person. The fact that he's black has nothing to do with it. I noticed that there wasn't a long line of white guys fighting for my affection, and I'm not going to let a prejudiced society keep me a spinster. It's easy for a happily married white couple to criticize me, but I have to live for myself, not for them."

Changing Social Patterns

Social patterns are one of the many factors in race relations in America. With the demise of Victorian moral standards in this country, we note an artificial and unprecedented emphasis on sex and a resultant breakdown in moral restraint. There is no question that unrestrained sexual activity has emerged from the shadows into the daylight of social acceptance. It is more often than not the theme of modern novels, especially romance novels. In fact, the language in many of these novels borders on pornography. They may be called "romance" novels, but explicit and sometimes abberative sex is not romance. Far too many television sitcoms and movies are nothing more than a mask for pornography to invade our living rooms. In some form or another, sex emblazons the cover of the majority of popular magazines. It is exploited in the sale of homes, household appliances, clothing, and autos.

The consequences of this erosion in morality are evidenced in an unprecedented rise in adult and teenage premarital, extramarital, and promiscuous sex activity. The increase in family breakups and divorce is alarming. Family ties and restraints are looser, in some cases nonexistent.

The "emancipated" teenager is the scourge of teachers, social workers, police officers, probation officers, and judges. There has been a startling rise in juvenile crimes and offenses, teenage pregnancies, venereal diseases, and in the general acceptance of adolescent premarital sexual intercourse. A social worker assigned to a wealthy California suburb documented a thirteen-year-old girl who had been given a contraceptive device and instructed in its use by "enlightened" and permissive parents.

The number of teenage fathers has more than tripled in the last 20 years. Efforts to curtail such activity have been virtually ineffective. Over two million babies are born each year to teenage mothers who are scarcely more than babies themselves. Some of these "emancipated," undisciplined, promiscuous youngsters get involved in interracial relationships. Some of these relationships develop into intermarriage, which gives legitimacy to the children. Distressingly, the chances of such marriages succeeding are quite low.

In one area of social change, we note a rise in religious and racial tolerance. We recognize that racial prejudice and discrimination are not disappearing overnight, however there is a definite degree of moderation. With the rise of protests and demands for civil rights and educational dialogue, progress will continue. The nation if not the world for generations to come will be indebted to the vision and sacrificial leadership and martyrdom of the late Dr. Martin Luther King, Jr. The violence, the deaths, and destruction spawned by racial prejudice and hatred taught Americans of all ethnicities that respect and tolerance for our mutual humanity are the pathways to peace. I extol love and would like to add it to the formula, but I'm not looking for love; I'll settle for respect.

We Americans of African ethnicity are not clamoring for love. What we want, yea demand, is equal opportunity to pursue our dreams and aspirations. I don't want to appear as "preacher" but hope is very much alive!

A poll conducted by a Protestant church in a New York suburb (with homes ranging from $150,000 to over $250,000) to determine whether an African-American family would welcome revealed these pertinent reactions:

Mr. H.... "I moved out here to get away from niggers.... When the first one moves out here, we're moving out!" This was an honest answer; certainly not the solution nor the consensus.

Mr. G.... was not as intractable. He admitted, "I know very little about Negroes, or should I say, black people. What I've heard is not all bad. I know that there are some very successful black persons, such as businessmen, professionals, and politicians.

"I'm a Christian and a patriot and I want to do the right thing." After a moment or two he continued, "As long as they are decent and can afford to live out here, I suppose it's all right."

Mrs. R.... had a real but not a fully factual concern.

"We worked hard and sacrificed and saved in order to buy this home," she confided, "And I for one don't want a bunch of poverty-stricken Negroes moving in, causing the property values to decrease."

I facetiously asked, "But how could a bunch of poverty-stricken Negroes or poor white folk who have no money or good credit buy any of these beautiful homes in this area?"

She appeared slightly confused as she wrinkled her brow and finally answered, "I guess you've got a point. I guess they couldn't, but I still don't want any Negroes living out here."

I then pointed out that statistics from a poll taken by realty boards and governmental agencies revealed that property values of integrated suburban areas have remained stable and in some cases actually risen. I further pointed out that any African-American family who could indeed afford to purchase property in the area would probably be an asset to the community.

After considering these facts, she moderated, "Well, if that's the actual truth, who am I to complain? After all, I'm not prejudiced."

I smiled and thanked her, but I really wanted to iterate, "Please dear lady, give me a break."

Getting back to the subject, what effect will moderating attitudes and increasing liberality have on interracial romantic relationships? The majority of pollsters discovered that homeowners in the suburbs were willing to live next to a stable black family, but opposed to interracial marriage. Others felt that if the number of black families were kept to a minimum there would be no problems.

Mr. B....an Italian-Catholic, partially-disabled Korean War veteran, father of three, in the real estate business, is well acquainted with the American brand of racial religious bigotry. When asked his opinion on black persons moving into a neighborhood, he gave these sobering comments.

"Why should I mind; they're American and human like the rest of us. Being a 'whop', I've been on the receiving end of prejudice all my life and I'm not about to give the 'business' to anyone else. Furthermore, I don't judge people on the basis of race but on their character." He continued, "I've got a lot of black friends who are welcome to my home anytime, and the neighbors who don't like it can go jump. A black buddy of mine saved my life when I took some shrapnel," pointing to his crippled leg, he continued, "Roscoe was really a great guy, I'll never forget him."

When asked his opinion on interracial marriage, he answered, "It really doesn't matter to me. It's none of my business whom anyone marries. If a white girl marries a black man, she's got to live with him. The best of luck to them. And then life is too short to worry about things like that."

Mr. B.'s attitude represents an exception to the rule, for even some of the most liberal white persons still disapprove and can be quite concerned about an unknown white female being in the company of an equally unknown black male. Despite society's firm disapproval, there is a decided trend toward moderation among the younger generation.

As the female reaches college age, the quest for the 'man of her dreams' intensifies. Earning a college degree is often secondary to some of these matrimony-minded young ladies.

Some coeds, failing to find Caucasian male companionship, turn to available males from other ethnic groups including African-Americans.

Most African-American male students realize that they must maintain exemplary behavior and so refrain from friendly overtures toward white females on campus. During my college days, if a white coed talked to me, I acknowledged the greeting but never proffered one.

On numerous occasions I was offered social invitations, which I politely refused for numerous reasons. First, I was in college to further my education. Second, I had such a difficult time in being admitted, I dared not jeopardize continuing my educational pursuits. Social interaction with white females was not a category of my goals.

Significantly, over three hundred interviews revealed that in college most social activities between black males and white females are initiated by the female.

Please note that while some of these relationships do indeed culminate in marriage, the vast majority dissolve as a "passing fancy." I certainly wouldn't want to alarm any reader by suggesting that his or her daughter will be thrown into some kind of promiscuous or unacceptable relationship with one of the few black students in attendance.

CHAPTER 7
Analysis of White Female Involved

Have you ever seen a black male and a white female walking together on the street, or sitting together in a restaurant, or lolling on a beach? What thought entered your mind? Were you angered or disgusted? Was what you saw offensive? Do you consider race mixing indecent or immoral?

A large percentage of white Americans firmly believe that race mixing is indecent and interracial marriage is morally wrong, and refer to the Holy Bible in an attempt to prove their contentions.

In the Old Testament, God prohibited Jews from marrying Gentiles or non-Jews on religious grounds, not because of race. Now if nonbelieving caucasians really believed that the statute applied to racial intermarriage, why then do so many of them not observe all the other laws and statutes included in the Ten Commandments? What hypocrisy.

When considering race mixing, they most likely think of a big over-sexed black "Buck" taking advantage of a helpless flower from the garden of womanhood, or of a low-class lustful black male consorting with a pitiably disturbed or unprincipled "white trash" female.

Though not personally affected by this situation, many white Americans are offended and disturbed. Some become so disturbed they actually will verbally insult and in some instances molest the couple; others become so angered, they resort to violence, especially against the objectional black male. Down through the blood-drenched history of America, a myriad of black males have been serious injured and even killed by irate white persons. Tragically, such acts are still being committed.

Whenever the subject of race mixing comes up, the question most often asked is, would you want your son or daughter to marry a black person? The daughter marrying a black person is of graver concern than a son, so I will pursue the probability of the daughter getting involved with a black male. Hopefully this is a hypothetical situation. What would you do, if your lovely daughter, the center of your fondest dreams for her success in life, were to bring home a black male and introduce him as the love of her life? What would you say? If this situation were to happen, and certainly, I could not criticize you for hoping that it doesn't, be reminded that it would not be unprecedented in the history of America. Tragic though it might be to you, it certainly would not be the last such relationship and perhaps would merely be a statistic in an increasing trend.

In a previous chapter I made reference to author Lester F. Ward's "four laws of race mixing." I here refute his second law, "The women of any race will vehemently reject the men of any race which they regard as lower than their own," white females and black females do not vehemently reject black males; some eagerly accept and even seek them. For certain, no black male could get involved with a white female if she weren't in favor of it.

During slavery, despite efforts to prevent it, there was considerable sexual activity between male slaves and white females. There was indeed ample opportunity for a male house servant and a neglected or sexually frustrated slave master's wife or daughter to come together in absence of the husband or father. A slave would not have dared to make an overture toward a white female, knowing full well that the penalty for such folly was death. Hence these liasons were initiated by the female, and the slave had no choice in the decision. In order to retain his "house" job as opposed to being a "fieldhand," and in order not to incur the displeasure or wrath of the propositioning female, he dared not refuse.

Consider this: the white mistress of the house literally held the slave's life in her hands. If perchance they were discovered, she had only to claim that the slave was raping her. She, a violated, helpless white woman, would be in the clear. He, the apprehended, adjudged guilty rapist, would be immediately hanged. What a quandary! The poor black slave was damned if he didn't and certainly doomed if caught. I can't understand, under such pressure, how in Heaven's name the pressured slave could have been aroused sufficiently to even effect sexual union, let alone complete it....

Since emancipation, many southern mixed race couples have been romantically involved and migrated to northern states to get married.

Why do white women associate with African-Americans? Why would a beautiful, cultured, educated white female get involved with and even fall in love with a black male? But even more, why would she go so far as to actually marry him? What motivations could possibly cause such a female to forsake her family and friends, even to suffer ostracism, to throw her lot with a black man?

As one charming lady expressed to her black fiance, "I'm willing to endure the consequences of my decision. I'm willing to suffer the ignominy of your race, just love me and tell me that you need me."

In order to find answers and to satisfy my own curiosity, I interviewed three hundred white females who were romantically involved with black men. Some were married and seemingly content. The interviewees ranged from 17 to 45 years of age and represented a cross-section of society ranging from the lowest socioeconomic level to the upper-middle-class. Educationally they ranged from fast-food cashier to private secretary; from unskilled factory worker to registered nurse; from college student to school teacher. Interestingly, one was a highly intelligent, beautiful, articulate lawyer who had fallen in love with a former convict. She bankrolled him in opening a successful restaurant. Strange, indeed, what "love" will do. The moral standards ranged from prostitute to devoted mother; from promiscuous thrill-seeker to Sunday school teacher.

The persons and their stories are real; the names are fictional for obvious reasons. I trust that you will not attempt to categorize all white females who get or are involved in an interracial relationship by these individuals and their case histories, for they represent only a nominal percentage of such cases in a large and complex composite.

Here is an interesting case. I got a call and an invitation to officiate at a wedding. I had known the black male caller for many years and was less than pleasantly surprised when he appeared at my office with an astonishingly beautiful white female to discuss particulars. After a series of questions the following information surfaced:

- The young lady came from an upper-middle-class, financially secure family. She was an only child and having problems with her parents. She had dropped out of college but was gainfully employed and making a good salary and had her own apartment. She drove a paid-for late-model car. My analysis was thus; she had a sense of low self-esteem. She was angry with her parents, whom she claimed showed her no affection and were more committed to their social status and financial success.

- The male had dropped out of school in the tenth grade, had no GED, and no interest in upgrading his education. He had a criminal record and had served time for petty crimes, which was a revelation to the young lady.

I asked him, "What do you do for a living? What kind of job do you have?"

He replied, "Ah washes cars."

"You can't earn enough money to support a household because when it's raining or snowing, you can't work. Is that correct?"

He responded, "So what, she makes plenty of money."

After a few questions, it was established that he had no bank account and just a few dollars in his pocket. The young lady was astonished. She stood up, looked straight at him, and with emotion tinging her voice she stated, "You haven't been honest with me. You've lied to me." Then addressing me. "Thanks a lot, Reverend, you've just opened my eyes. I was about to make the mistake of my life."

They left the office and drove away in her auto. I saw them no more.

The questionnaire used in this treatise as follows:

AGE: _____

NAME: Fictitious _____

BACKGROUND

A. Education

    1. Highest grade completed _____

    2. Reason for not completing _____

    3. Degrees _____

    4. Specialized training _____

B. Home Life

    City, State (Rural) _____

    1. Mother relationship _____

    2. Father relationship _____

    3. Brother, sister relationship _____

    4. Church relationship _____

    5. Culture _____

       a. National or ethnic origin _____

       b. Languages spoken in home _____

       c. Music, art, literature _____

C. Vocation

    1. Type of work _____

    2. Length of employment _____

    3. History _____

    4. Future plans _____

D. Interests

    1. Athletics _____

    2. Hobbies _____

    3. Pets _____

    4. Prior romantic interests _____

E. Present Romantic Interest

    1. Marital   Yes _____ No _____

    2. Introduction to Negroes _____

    3. Feelings about Negroes (Prior) _____

BACKGROUND OF MALE INVOLVED

A. Education

    1. Highest grade completed _____

    2. Reason for not completing _____

    3. Degrees _____

    4. Specialized training _____

B. Vocation

    1. Type of work _____

    2. Length of employment _____

    3. History _____

    4. Future plans _____

C. Interests

    1. Athletics _____

    2. Hobbies _____

    3. Pets _____

    4. Prior romantic interests _____

CHARACTER OF MALE INVOLVED

A. Personality traits

    1. Kind _____ Brutal _____

    2. Unselfish Domineering _____

    3. Demonstratively affectionate Yes _____ No _____

    4. Warm _____ Cold _____

    5. Happy _____ Morose _____

    6. Understanding _____ Biased _____

7. Well-adjusted _____ Disturbed _____

B. Moral Traits

    1. Honest _____

    2. Dependable _____

    3. Does he drink? _____ (Moderately _____ Excessively _____)

    4. Use Profanity? _____

    5. Religious _____

    6. Attend Church (Regularly) _____

    7. Has he ever suggested or performed an unnatural sex act with you? _____ (Asked only of promiscuous females)

ROUTINE

1. Do you find Negroes more affectionate than whites? _____

_____

2. Do you feel Negroes have more sex appeal? _____

_____

3. Is the Negro's color attractive? _____

_____

4. Does his color excite you sexually? _____

_____

5. Are you more comfortable with Negroes or whites? _____

_____

6. Do Negroes make you feel appreciated and wanted? _____

_____

7. Do Negroes make you feel superior? _____

_____

8. Are you satisfied _____ Disappointed _____ with your present romantic interest?

9. If your present mate were to leave you or die, would you seek another Negro mate? _____

_____

10. How do your parents feel? _____

_____

11. How does this affect you?_____

_____

12. How do you feel about society's regard for you? _____

_____

13. What are your plans for the future? _____

_____

"You must admit, any white woman who has anything to do with a Negro needs her head examined!" exclaimed a white man who considered himself devoid of prejudice.

I retorted, "I don't admit any such thing." However, I recognize this opinion and generally conclude that any white female involved with a black person is demonstrating an abnormal pattern, which may not be without basis in some cases. I also found that many of these females were intelligent, personable, well-adjusted, perfectly satisfied, and firmly resolved in and with their choice.

Not being a psychiatrist or psychologist, I could not scientifically isolate neurotic and psychotic patterns. However, for the sake of classification, I will use these terms with reservation and contrast behavior patterns in the light of normal and abnormal manifestations.

Normal Drives

We must recognize in view of statistics that there are scores of white females involved with black males who are motivated by the female's ordinate desire and need for a mate, which is a normal drive. The fact that their mate happens to be African-American is incidental and no reflection on the lady's normalcy.

Barbara…beautiful, intelligent, self-reliant, the well-adjusted only child of wealthy, loving parents, felt that she had been given everything parents could give a child—warmth, love and understanding. She met Donald…at an airport lunch counter while returning to college for her senior year. She asserted, "I was fascinated by Donalds' rich brown skin color, well-trimmed mustache, and deep resonant voice from the very start."

Her father failed in intimidating her by threatening to disinherit her. He then offered Donald ten thousand dollars to sever their relationship. When Donald refused, her father then threatened violence. As a last resort he swore out a warrant for her arrest as a mental incompetent. When the psychiatrist ruled her perfectly sane, he promptly disowned and disinherited her. She was baffled at her father's unreasonable hatred of Donald and at his complete lack of understanding and sympathy toward her.

Barbara and Donald have been married three years and are happy, despite her family's rejection. Barbara completed college and is employed as a receptionist-secretary. Donald is employed in electronics in a first-rate industrial plant. They are childless but plan starting a family in the near future. They live in an upscale suburban neighborhood in their own beautiful home and get along well with their neighbors and are quite content.

Some women associate with African-Americans because of a lack of available or eligible white males. And of course, some of the mixed race associations culminate in marriage. In an earlier chapter I mentioned that women outnumber men in this country. In geographical areas where there is a preponderant amount of females and a scarcity of males, with some of the males being African-Americans, there may be some degree of race mixing.

Circumstances such as wars and national emergencies can be a significant factor in inter-race mixing. During World War II, the Vietnam War, and the Korean War, there were upsurges in race mixing on the continent and abroad. The mobility of troops in various areas exposed African-American soldiers to white females who had no previous contact with African-Americans. On the European continent any "Yank" white or black was at a premium, so naturally, black GI's took full advantage of the situation. Some of these wartime associations resulted in some race mixing. Many of the relationships developed into serious romances, culminating in marriages which brought "war brides" to the States. We've all read of and are aware of the thousands of "brown babies" that resulted from the more promiscuous unions.

Here on the home front, the continuing induction of males and females into the armed services have and will contribute to race mixing both here and abroad. Our second son, Gordon, a career serviceman stationed in Europe, married a lovely English lady. They have one daughter (Maria, our precious granddaughter, who is a joy to behold). Many African-American servicemen stationed overseas discover that they are eagerly sought after by white and black females alike. They may some have some problems; a white female holding the arm of a black service man remarked, "Six months ago if a black man had touched me, my flesh would have crawled. But here I am in love with a wonderful black man and loving it."

I recall my own situation during World War II. I was exempt because I was attending a theological college. There were few males attending, and the fact that I was African-American didn't exempt me from the overtures of numerous white females. I was perceptive enough to realize that my popularity with the ladies was due entirely to the fact that I was an available male and not to some dubious irresistible charm I may have possessed. Under normal circumstances I perhaps would have generated only a casual interest because of my ethnic origin.

However, integration of the races in schools, colleges, industry, and public recreation facilities has contributed to the interracial picture. I must agree with the segregationist's point of view: "School integration results in social integration, and social integration contributes to the race mixing complex." White youngsters learning together with blacks in the classroom during the day, socializing with them during recess and after school, mingling with them at athletic games, dances, and other school functions, occasionally may result in some becoming romantically involved.

Janette met and became attracted to Roy in high school and married him shortly after graduation. She comes from a family of modest means; her father is a bus driver, her mother clerks in a department store. During her school years the family rented the first floor unit of a duplex in an area that was deteriorating. Her parents became increasingly distressed as African-Americans moved into the area, and they finally moved to a low-rent, all-white neighborhood. They bitterly opposed her friendship with Roy and after their marriage refused to have anything to do with her.

Both she and Roy realized that he was vocationally unprepared to take on the responsibilities of marriage. Roy plans to pursue vocational training in the near future. Otherwise, Janette has no regrets in marrying Roy. They are sustained, despite her parent's objections, by their mutual love and devotion and are optimistic about the future.

Martha, twenty-one, beautiful, and mentally sharp, is an unusual story. Georgia-born and reared, she has fond memories of black governesses and many fond memories of black playmates on her father's farm. After attending segregated schools through high school, she chose to come north to college. She was a member of the cheerleading squad, an honor student, and a popular sorority sister. She met Robert, a brilliant senior with dark, but not handsome, features. After graduation they were married. They regularly attend an integrated church where they were married, and have a host of friends both white and black.

They are progressive, productive, and happy despite being childless. Robert, ambitious and resourceful, owns a successful real estate business which he started while in college.

This case had an interesting implication; Martha was attacked by a black male one dark night in a parking lot of a shopping mall. Her screams frightened off her assailant. She was roughed up, frightened, and her purse was stolen, but she was not seriously injured.

I asked her if this experience in any way affected her thoughts about African-Americans.

"Not in the least," she explained. "Any intelligent person knows that all black men aren't rapists and robbers; I just happened to run into one that was. There are thousands of white deviants and rapists. It'll be unintelligent for me to consider all white men as such. It is foolish to judge the mass by acts of an individual; there are good and bad in all groups. And then I've known too many good and kind persons of color in my experiences."

I considered her approach refreshing, logical, and rational. Integration in industry provides a climate for the possibility for race mixing (I emphasize possibility over inevitability). Regrettably, far too many African-Americans have been denied employment because of the fear of this possibility that has been magnified far out of proportion.

Being aware of this fear, I once used a little reverse psychology on a discriminatory and prejudiced employer. I answered by telephone a newspaper want ad and was told that the job was still open and to come immediately. Upon arriving, I was ushered into the boss's office. I cited the reason for my visit. Without hesitation the boss told me quite firmly that I didn't qualify for the job. I explained that I had a number of years experience and was an excellent machine operator. I even offered to work one day without pay in order to prove that I was qualified. He was adamant, refusing to even give me a chance to prove myself.

I was certain that the reason for my disqualification was my dark skin. So I pressed from another angle, explaining, "Sir, if you are afraid that I might be interested in some of the white ladies employed here, your fears are unfounded. I'm not the least interested in white women. In fact, I don't consider white women any more desirable than women of color. I need a job; I'm not afraid of work; I don't drink, lay off or disturb the help; I'm punctual, dependable, and honest.... And I reiterate, I'm not the least bit interested in white ladies."

His countenance immediately changed. "You mean to say that you don't want a white lady?"

"That's absolutely right, sir." I declared, "I'm not in the least bit interested in romance; I'm interested in finance."

A smile tinged his face as he proffered his hand, which of course I shook. "Well, if that's how it is, by

God, I would never have believed it, a nigger who doesn't want a white woman."

As a rule, wise black males working where white females are employed in order to keep their jobs will be cordial and polite but distant.

Many friendly white women, being unaware of this and of the pressures on the black employee, often can't understand a fellow's aloofness and ultra-politeness toward them. Some females out of simple friendliness or a desire to demonstrate a lack of prejudice will conduct themselves in a way that can be misconstrued by resentful white males, which can compound the black male's problems....

Many genuinely friendly and innocent overtures have caused helpless black males to lose their jobs because some prejudiced boss misconstrued the advances a the prelude to race mixing.

Bob, who had worked on his job for over nine years and had suffered many indignities at the hands of abusive and prejudiced fellow workers, was placed in a precarious predicament by the friendliness of a white female worker. Approached and accused of being too friendly to her, he was attacked and severely beaten by two males. The police were called, they summoned an ambulance, and Bob was taken to the hospital. He stayed overnight and was released to the custody of the police department. Unable to make bond after being charged with assault, Bob appeared before a judge, who fined him and gave him a 90-day suspended sentence with a warning. Needless to say, Bob was terminated. What a price he paid!

I was once employed in a large dry cleaning plant where white females worked alongside African-American males. We pressed the clothes and then hung the finished garments on racks. The females checked and assembled them so they were ready for the customer. Consequently we were in constant communication. During our coffee breaks and during lunch we chatted and enjoyed a noncommittal fellowship, which offended some of the white male workers. After these whites complained to the boss and threatening to walk out, the boss fired all black males. I learned a lesson that I never forgot.

Betty, plain but personable, an intelligent high school graduate, met Ben in a large manufacturing plant where both were employed. One rainy night she missed her ride and asked Ben for a lift. He reluctantly complained, explaining that if any of the white males saw them, his job would be in jeopardy. On the way Ben explained the "Negro problem" and cautioned her against talking to him or being too friendly to him in the plant or in the presence of other whites.

Having had no previous exposure to white race prejudice, she ignored his advice and unwisely sought and talked with him in the plant. Their relationship blossomed into a full-blown romance. On occasion she championed Ben's case when other employees spoke desparagingly about him and their relationship. Someone wrote a letter to the personnel manager, who terminated Ben. Ben didn't follow his own advice to his detriment. Betty was warned to discontinue seeing Ben upon threat of termination. She refused to be intimidated and promptly joined the ranks of the unemployed. After Ben found employment, they were married.

I asked her what attracted her to Ben, who was not a very handsome man. She said she was drawn by his deep, melodious voice, his pleasing personality, and his buoyant spirit. These reasons were, of course, valid but we can't rule out propinquity, which affords individuals a chance to get to know each other.

I wondered and inquired how her parents regarded her marriage to a Black man.

She responded with a twinge of emotion in her voice, "The nightmare has become a reality for my racist father. He threatened to kill Ben, and has had nothing to do with me since. He forbids me to come to the home to visit my mother, who likes Ben." She added, "Ben works hard, is thrifty, and is a wonderful and devoted husband who loves me dearly."

She lost some of her former friends, but has many new ones in the neighborhood where they live, and has no regrets.

Dances, nightclubs and bars provide opportunity for whites and blacks to meet and socialize. In an atmosphere of frivolity under the spell of seductive music and soft lights, alcohol-influenced fun-seeking whites and blacks can get together.

I wondered what could possibly motivate a young lady so extremely attractive and personable as Marjorie to get involved with James. She comes from a middle-class family broken by divorce. She attended an integrated school, but had little to do with African-Americans attending there. Upon graduation she left home, took up residence in a distant city, dated regularly, and was happy.

At the invitation of some female friends she attended a "rock 'n roll" party where she was introduced to African-Americans in a different setting. She liked what she saw and before the evening was over was enjoying dancing with uninhibited blacks.

Marjorie confessed, "The warmth and lack of inhibition of the partygoers impressed me. I had never known such warmth and demonstration of affection from anyone that I experienced there. They didn't know anything about me, they just accepted me for who I am."

She and James have been married four years and have a most beautiful and darling multiracial daughter. Her father, who was strongly opposed and wanted nothing to do with her and James, fell in love with his sweet little granddaughter and dotes on her. It is significant that the gurgling smile of a precious infant can erase racial barriers and can bring humans together where preaching has failed.

One of the most fascinating confessions came from Alabama-born, nightclub singer and stripper Sharrie. She was long-limbed, shapely, and excitingly beautiful with even white teeth, shining dark hair, deep brown eyes and personality plus. She should have been in Hollywood. She could have attracted and gotten any man she wanted, but prefers black males. She called, requesting that I officiate at her marriage to a black male.

Here is her story as she related it: "As a child, black people were just part of the scenery. We kept to ourselves and they kept to themselves. They did all the menial work, served us, and socially kept their distance. They knew their place and stayed in it. Sure, I was friendly with them. I talked and joked with them, but frankly, never thought of them in any other role."

At age eighteen she left home and migrated north, ending up in New York City. She did a variety of odd jobs—fry-cook, waitress, elevator operator, and finally, just for kicks, applied for a job as a stripper in a "strip joint." I encouraged her to continue her story.

"I was just a 'green', but I got the job because I was a 'looker'. I worked the 'strip' circuit for about three years and made good money."

I inquired about her romantic life. She met and dated all kinds of males, was not interested prostitution, but found no romance.

I probed. "Did you really expect to find romance in such a setting?"

"Sure. Who knows what the future will bring. With all those guys coming around, I hoped to find the right one. What girl doesn't?"

"But do decent guys patronize strip shows? On occasion, I've checked some out of curiosity. All I saw were boozehounds, guys looking to escape from the "old lady," guys looking for a make; looking for 'flesh' for sale, 'look' freaks. Never the right guy. I changed the subject. "Did you consider black guys?"

"Oh, yeah, I came in contact with a lot of black guys. You know, there are a lot of black people in show business. They work around night clubs and many are patrons, but I wasn't interested."

She pondered for a moment before continuing. "Then my whole life changed. It's still hard for me to understand. You see, I was stripping in this club out east. Everything was integrated in the show; the band, the personnel, the patrons. The first night I came on, I noticed this black drummer. He was so cool, so versatile. His cuing was just perfect, which means a lot to a stripper, if you know what I mean. After the show, I commented on his skill and on how much he helped my act.

He was gracious—and attractive—and his deep baritone voice excited me. All that night and the next night, I kept thinking of him. Now this is what I couldn't understand or get out of my mind—I longed to touch his black satiny skin. I wanted to embrace him and him to embrace me. The more I thought of it, the more it excited me. This was the guy I wanted! And I didn't give a damn that he was black!"

She seemed to be unwinding, which is not at all unusual for many who are at a crossroads in their lives and just need someone to listen. I drew her out.

"The next night after work, I cornered him. He seemed friendly enough but that was all. I tried every trick I knew, but I couldn't break his composure. He proved to be a master at parrying, evasion, circumventing the subject and politely changing it. He was driving me crazy. He haunted my dreams at night and filled my waking thoughts. While working, I was actually putting on the show for him but he confined his attention wholly to his drumming. My white thighs, partially exposed buttocks, bumps and grinds didn't faze him. But I didn't give up."

I was amused and asked, "Did you finally get him?"

"Oh, yes, I finally got him. On our first date, I just grabbed him and kissed him, hard. Evidently, he could resist me no longer; he kissed me hungrily, passionately. I knew then that he wanted me as much as I wanted and needed him. On our third date, I stayed all night with him; it was wonderful. His hands caressed my body; his voiced wooed me as I had never been wooed before. He kissed me with a fiery passion, then tenderly, then possessively. I knew and experienced an excitement, an ecstasy, I never thought possible. From that night on I was his completely. I just couldn't get enough of him.

My decision was made. He was the man for me and I was going to marry him."

It was unnecessary for me to prod. She talked and I just sat and listened.

"My family doesn't approve but I don't care what my family or anyone else thinks, or the whole world for that matter. I've found my man. He loves me and I love him and no one is going to come between us. I know in my heart that what I'm doing is right."

I broke in, "What's his name? I know a lot about him but you haven't mentioned his name."

She smiled. "Please forgive me, his name is Carl." She continued her narration. "I'm not stripping anymore. He says he doesn't want to share me with anyone. He has overlooked my past and just wants me to be his wife and mother of our children."

I asked, "Why did you come to Minnesota?"

"We heard that Minnesota was a liberal state as far as race relations are concerned and has a lot of job opportunities. We're happy here. We've applied for our marriage license and have to wait five days to pick it up. Will you marry us even though we aren't members of your church? We'll pay whatever you charge."

We set a date and a few days later I performed the ceremony, encouraged them to attend our church services and bade them Godspeed.

In my survey I questioned several females who considered the skin color of African-Americans attractive in contrast to the colorlessness of so called "white" skin. These ladies used such superlatives such as "exotic," "fascinating," "exciting," delightfully "brown."

"I find brown people intriguing. I just love to touch that smooth brown skin," Beverly voiced.

"I just don't like white skin; it looks so lifeless. I don't even like my own skin color. That's why I try to get a tan, even thought I know the sun is not good for me," complained Pam.

"I go for that smooth brown skin. You people look more virile and masculine," testified Clarice.

Redhaired, freckle-faced Esther abhorred her freckles and was displeased that she couldn't get a tan. She remarked, "I really like Negroes' color; there are so many shades. My guy looks like a bronzed Greek god. I just love his color."

My analysis may be based upon a psychological/ biological factor, but reality can't be ignored. Many persons cannot resist the urge to touch a freshly painted surface that has a warning sign "Do not touch. FRESH PAINT." Curiously, the human creatures desire is often excited or incited by curiosity and/or prohibition. Forbidden fruit has a special appeal. Parents who severely and constantly criticize and denigrate black people in the presence of their daughters may or can be instrumental in generating a curiosity and a desire to investigate.

Twenty-year-old Linda, a voluptuous, attractive blond expressed, "My father was almost fanatical in his hatred for black people." She was concerned whether we preferred to be called Negro or black or colored. I assured her that there is no preference as far as I was concerned. She continued. "He used to drive us through the Negro ghetto and point out the squalor and deterioration, claiming that this was dramatic and conclusive evidence of the Negro's genetic inferiority. He delighted in calling our attention to some unbathed, dirty, ill-kempt drunk. He repeatedly warned us not to have anything to do with Negro males because they are potential rapists."

I listened attentively and encouraged her to expound.

"I knew my father's predilection was unreasonable because I knew and met a number of your people in high school and college. They came from good families and were good students. I knew that what our father was attempting to do was not honest. Out of curiosity I began dating a black fellow and found him congenial, personable, and warm."

I queried how her father reacted to her associating with black persons. She said that her father found out about her relationship with her boyfriend and followed her one night. He fearfully beat her boyfriend and warned him never to see her again under threat of his life. He then had her picked up by the authorities in order to throw a scare into her. The authorities questioned her, warned her to have nothing more to do with black people, and released her. These measures failed. Despite her father's disapproval, she and her male friend left town and ended up in Minnesota. They are both employed, live together, and plan to be married.

Neurotic Drives

There are many seriously disturbed white females involved with black males who are motivated by uni-dentifiable neurotic drives. Distressingly, they add to the mounting statistics of unwed mothers, narcotic addicts, and prostitutes. Neurotic girls who feel insecure, unloved, and unsure of their self-worth and who are unable to deal with such problems seek an escape. Some turn to drugs, some resort to committing criminal acts, still others turn to promiscuous sex.

Sue…sought an escape by getting involved with black males. When I interviewed her, she blurted out her story. "I'm a streetwalker but I need the money. You know, a good prostitute can make a lots of money."

"What are your plans for the future?"

"I want to be respected, get a good job—I'm an excellent typist. I want to find a good man who will marry me and raise a family."

I asked how she expected to find a "good" man by working as a prostitute, risking her health and her life.

She surprisingly confessed, "I admit, I'm confused. I hate what I'm doing; I despise myself. Yet I get a thrill out of men desiring me, using me, then paying me.

Sometimes I get as much as a hundred dollars for one 'trick' for about an hour's work." One fool actually gave me three hundred dollars. What I really don't understand is that I give most of my money to Mitch (her pimp, who like a loathsome parasite exploits these disturbed and vulnerable females). "I know he is just taking advantage of me. And I can't understand it, but I just love the guy."

I inquired into her background. Her father died when she was quite young; her mother was unkind to her, deserted her when she was in elementary school and ended up serving time in prison. She was raised by her grandmother, who fortunately was financially able to provide for her. She had a difficult and unpleasant childhood. She ran away from home and ended up hustling on the streets of Minneapolis, Minnesota, where she got involved with Mitch. I gave Mitch one hundred dollars and fifty dollars to Sue for the interview.

I remind you, I'm not a psychiatrist; these are my personal conclusions arrived at after analyzing her bizarre behavior. The death of her father was certainly not a deliberate desertion, but to a young, impressionable girl it could easily have been interpreted as such. Of, course her mother's act was. Consequently, she felt abandoned by the two most important and dearest people in her young life. She could understandably hate her parents consciously. It is respectable to hate one's parents, therefore, without being aware of it; her need for a male love relationship very likely had its roots in a feeling of guilt stemming from her hatred of her parents. Unconsciously, she well could have felt, she deserved to be punished, but there were no parents to administer it. So her unconscious mind could further have equated her relationships with various men as a substitute form of punishment.

Psychological studies of this phenomenon have significantly linked the two reactions—a sense of guilt and an apparent masochisms factor involved in prostitution. Further, she possibly counterfeited the emotion of "love" to her sexual partners, who in their need for sex gave her a feeling of deep-seated revenge against her father for deserting her.

The money she earned fulfilled an unconscious belief that money is the ultimate attainment of human desire, as so many are so deluded. But in her case, the money being tainted, she rejected this concept, so she willingly gave it to her pimp, Mitch, who was the symbol of the source of love she so desperately needed.

Toni…is a neurotic thrill-seeker and makes an interesting case study. Her mother had received reports that her delinquent daughter was somewhere in the "Negro ghetto" and came to me soliciting my aid in finding her. With information supplied to me through the "grapevine," I successfully located her.

I along with the mother and two police officers went to a dilapidated apartment building in the area. As we entered, we mounted a dimly lit stairway leading to the second floor with trepidation; what could we hope to find? The police officer's presence was reassuring. As we gained the top of the stairs, an ill-kempt burly black male came out of an apartment door, glowered at us, puffed nervously on a cigarette, and quickly ran down the stairs into the night.

We located the room down the dark hallway. One of the officers knocked repeatedly on the door, demanding, "Open the door in the name of the law!" No response. He repeated his demand, then nodded to me. I called out, "This is Pastor LeRoy Gardner of North Central Baptist Church. No one is gong to hurt you. We're here to help you." The door slowly opened, revealing the disheveled, frightened daughter. She was scantily clad in a bra and panties. She was in desperate need of a bath. Her hair was a mess and there was an expression of surprise and dismay on her face.

The mother rushed past me emitting an anguished cry, pummeling the girl with clenched fists, and hurling invectives. "You no-good slut! What have you been doing with these filthy niggers?" The police officer separated them and quieted the mother.

The teenager was alone. Perhaps the black male whom we had met on the stairs was her captor, but he was long gone.

After calming the mother, the police officer questioned the young lady for information about the male involved. She defiantly refused to even give his name. She was allowed to go home with her mother with a word of warning to stay out of that area. The police had no basis to make an arrest and we left the premises. Despite the warning, the disturbed young lady returned to the apartment the next day, where I found her after receiving a telephone call from her mother.

I gave her twenty-five dollars for an interview. She was seventeen and had been delinquent the last two years. During that time she had run away from home numerous times and been involved with black people for about a year. I was curious as to how she came into contact with African-Americans. What follows is the scenario: She, along with some fellow delinquents came into the "Ghetto" seeking a new "thrill" as she put it. They met some black males in a bar. They picked out the males of their choice and went to an apartment, where they spend the night in illicit lovemaking. How stupid. But such activity is not unusual in this morally bankrupt society. She decided not to return home.

Despite her parents' disapproval and the police officer's warning, she was firm in her decision to continue living in the promiscuous and illegitimate relationship with her black lover. She was totally ignorant of the far-reaching consequences of such folly, placing not only herself in jeopardy but also her lover who could have, if caught, been charged with carnal knowledge and sent to prison for a number of years.

She stated emphatically, "I hate my father and will not live in his house anymore." She described her father, a successful businessman, as bigoted, brutal, and a notorious liar who had sexually abused her since she was nine years old. Her mother lacked courage, was docile and submissive to her father, and cold, possessive, and unloving toward her. No wonder Toni was motivated by neurotic needs.

I was unsuccessful in getting her and her male friend to even come to church, and abandoned them to their dilemma.

One day, Ricardo...brought Connie in for an interview. Connie was twenty years of age, attractive, vocal, intelligent, an ex-convict, and unquestionably emotionally disturbed. She quit high school in the tenth grade at the age of sixteen and has been delinquent since. After numerous encounters with the law, she was sentenced for shoplifting, served ninety days, and was released on parole which she broke.

While in confinement she was told of a black male who provided quarters, food, and refuge for fugitives and run aways. She successfully located Ricardo, and there they were.

Ricardo was a pimp and promptly used her as a streetwalker. She kept 50 percent of her earnings and Ricardo got 50 percent, which was unusual because in most cases the pimp gets the lion's share. Connie was definitely confused as to her future, failing to realize that prostitution is unproductive and often dangerous. Far too many prostitutes' bodies have been found and the cases continue unsolved.

I offered my assistance in dealing with her probation officer, which she flatly refused. Years earlier I had appeared in Ricardo's behalf in a court case, which he won, so he accepted no fee for himself or Connie for the interview. This was one case in which the old adage, "Cast your bread upon the water and after many days it will return," proved true.

I was introduced to Karen with these words: "This is Karen. She can get you anything you need." Bob, her heavily built, intimidating appearing, dark-skinned lover and "contact man," continued, "Just give her your size. She can supply you with suits, shirts, sport coats, anything you want."

I didn't hesitate to inform Bob that I wasn't interested in "hot" merchandise and that I didn't encourage criminals in their illegal activities. He didn't appreciate my criticism, but agreed to permit the interview for a payment of one hundred dollars. After I paid him, he smiled and thanked me. It is interesting how a hundred-dollar bill can quell the spirit of umbrage.

Karen was twenty-six, petite, blond and blue-eyed, charming and poised, with the physical attributes of a Hollywood starlet. She spoke with rapidity and expression.

Her conversation jumped from bragging to confession. She seemed, as is the case with many criminals, to get a morbid pleasure in discussing her criminal exploits.

Almost as a confession, she revealed that her career began by snitching "goodies" at the corner grocery store and shortly after that graduated to pilfering from her mother's purse. During adolescence her friends introduced her to "shoplifting" from department stores. Quitting high school at age sixteen, she was caught stealing and placed on probation. Continuing her criminal activities, she was caught again, sentenced, and served two-years in a woman's reformatory. After being released she joined a gang of lesbian boosters. As she described it, "The pickin's were good, the money came easy and the livin' was great!"

I inquired why and how she got involved with a black male, and she pointed out, "I may be a thief but I'm no homo."

One of the "dykes" as she referred to the ones who assume the male role in such relationships, had been trying for months to force her into an unnatural affair. One night under pressure from the dykes and in desperation, she leaped from their car and ran into the nearest bar—which was frequented by African-Americans. The lesbians boldly ran after and attempted to assault her.

A scuffle ensued that ended when Bob, a tall, full-back type, came to her aid and chased the lesbians out. He invited her to a booth and ordered a drink, which was gratefully received. After explaining her predicament and at Bob's invitation, she agreed to spend the night at his apartment.

I asked, "Why would you accept a strange black man's invitation to go to his apartment? Weren't you afraid of being taken advantage of? Weren't you just a little apprehensive?"

"Not especially. I needed help, bad; the dykes were mean and vicious. I knew the score, I wasn't a virgin, and Bob was a real man with something hanging between his legs, if you know what I mean. Further, I carry a twenty-two pistol and I'll use it if I have to."

I was convinced that she really meant that. I then asked, "Didn't the fact that he was black mean anything?"

"Oh, I thought about it, but really it didn't seem too important at the time. I was already in trouble. And I liked Bob right off the bat. What did I have to lose, and then the prospects were exciting."

I inquired into her family's views on the race issue.

"My parents are good, in fact sometimes too good; too strict. They belong to the Seventh Day Adventist church—you can't smoke; can't drink; can't go to dances. In fact they don't even eat meat. I have two sisters and a brother and they went for that insanity; not me. I'm not going to any church; I wanna be me and live my life the way I want to. Getting back to my parents, they taught us that everyone is equal in the sight of God regardless of color, but we weren't to have anything to do with Negroes. They felt that Negro boys would rape us. What hyprocrisy, as though white men don't rape."

She confessed that she knew this wasn't true because she knew a number of black students in her classes at school. She mentioned one boy who was very popular; a star on the basketball team. The girls, black and white, were crazy about him. However, during this time, she had no interest in or close association with any of them. She had no firm plans for the future; no prospects or interest in marriage or in establishing a home. She definitely planned to continue her criminal activities and provide the luxuries of life for herself. Apparently she was successful, judging by the expensive clothes she was wearing.

Candy...is a prostitute. Her story is stark and brutal, approaching incredulity. She had been raped by her father at age thirteen. This incestuous relationship continued for about six months, when she became pregnant. When her condition became obvious she was forced to reveal the truth to her mother.

When her mother confronted her father—in a fit of rage—he viciously beat her and her mother. The father was subsequently arrested, convicted, and sentenced to prison. Her parents are now divorced.

When the baby was born, in order to protect it the mother proceeded to raise the child as her own. Candy became sexually promiscuous, quit school at age sixteen, and started associating with a black male named Pretty Jack, who introduced her to prostitution.

Pretty Jack is tall and mustachioed with dark, distinctly handsome features. He is a fastidious dresser wearing expensive suits and jewelry and driving a late-model Cadillac. He acts as the procurer, receiving the money from her clients in advance. Candy meets the client at a location agreed upon. According to Pretty Jack, this practice protects him from entrapment by the police.

Candy is satisfied with Pretty Jack but frankly admits she doesn't love him; it's just a business arrangement. She confesses that she has never been in love, at least not what is extolled in song and verse. She recognizes the incestuous experiences with her father could conceivably have a direct bearing on her delinquency and promiscuity. She admits to actually despising men, gets no gratification from her sexual activities other than using men and extracting as much money from them as possible.

Here is an interesting dichotomy; she endeavors to faithfully attend morning Mass after plying her licentious trade during the night. Her thinking was decidedly confused, indicative of misunderstanding the enormity of her sin. When I asked how she could reconcile a sincere confession with continued sexual commission, she flippantly replied, "Oh, the priest always forgives me." This practice is non-Biblical because only God can forgive sin. This is also a supreme paradox; devoutly religious yet decidedly immoral.

She is aware that Pretty Jack is under surveillance

by the police and could eventually be arrested. After being arrested several times herself, she is bafflingly unconcerned about further arrests. An occasional stay in the county workhouse, which she amusingly refers to as the "rest-house" breaks up the routine and affords her a much needed rest.

Her haunting fear is that she will contract cancer of the cervix or the uterus, rendering her unfit to carry on the trade. Amazingly, she has no fear of death, feeling secure that God loves her and cares for her.

I regret that I could not help her, being neither a Catholic priest nor a Christ. The dear young lady is seriously confused, emotionally disturbed, and in desperate need of help. Her future is as dark as her past is sordid.

Ethel is a neurotic sexpot with an abnormal sex drive bordering on nymphomania. Everything about her, from her loosely bouncing coiffure to the provocative sway of her shapely hips, flaunts sex. She is outstandingly beautiful with bright expressive blue eyes, full sensuous lips, and a warm, husky voice, and she knows it. The word modesty is not in her vocabulary. Her appearance belies her emotional and mental turmoil.

Upon hearing that I was a sympathetic minister receptive to helping solve the problems of white females involved with black males, she came to me seeking help. She revealed that she had attempted suicide and threatened another attempt if I were unsuccessful in preventing her male friend from leaving her. All through our interview she continued her flirtatious mannerisms which I construed as being more affectacious than serious.

Ethel's background began with her illegitimate birth. She had no knowledge of her parents, having been adopted at a tender age by a prejudiced, ultra-religious couple who gave her material things, including a generous allowance, but denied her love and understanding. Obviously her problems began during her formative years. During her teens she was forbidden to attend parties, movies, or dances; could read no romance novels; wear no makeup and date no boys. She could associate with youths that her foster parents approved of. As she put it, "I felt like I was in a cage."

At this stage in her development, she needed direction and discipline administered with copious amounts of love and understanding, not harsh and unrealistic restrictions. Feeling stifled and being denied opportunity for self-expression and freedom to develop her natural abilities, she rebelled.

After her parents retired for the night, Ethel would oftimes slip out of the house and attend dances and house parties, ride around in cars with "emancipated" teens, use illegal drugs, and indulge in sexual activities. She attributed her popularity to her willingness to grant sexual favors.

Her parents eventually discovered her nightly sojourns, attributing her antisocial behavior to her inherited "bad blood" which further alienated her. Deeply hurt, dismayed, discouraged, misunderstood, and feeling unwanted and unloved, she ran away. She began associating with undisciplined and antisocial individuals.

In defiance of her parents and society, she started frequenting bars patronized by African-Americans. There she found even greater popularity as the young black males fawned upon her. Needless to say, she found disfavor with the black females and had an occasional confrontation bordering on violence. But she was unafraid.

Her suicidal tendency interested me; I questioned her at length. Once she put her head in an oven and turned on the gas but couldn't endure the smell of fumes and abandoned the effort. On another occasion she took a bottle of sleeping pills, but was discovered and hospitalized in time. She spent two weeks in the psychiatric ward. In my opinion she was released too soon. Because of her suicidal tendencies, she is potentially dangerous to herself and needs immediate and extensive psychiatric treatment.

As I mentioned before, this pitiable young lady had an inordinate sexual appetite, indulging in intercourse three or four times a day. She didn't consider herself a nymphomaniac inasmuch as she reach a climax each time. Interestingly, she had no interest in prostitution, considering it immoral. Curiously, she considered her sexual desires natural and God-ordained, hence its gratification could not be immoral or sinful. Her male friend couldn't match her sexual fever and threatened to leave her, which occasioned her visit to me.

She proved to be confused, frustrated, and seriously emotionally disturbed. In such an emotional state, happiness in the foreseeable future for Ethel is indeed very dim. I proved of no help to her as she rejected my counsel with the retort, "I've wasted my time coming to you. You're just another religious square!"

Conclusions

There are myriad and complex reasons for white females getting involved with and marrying African-Americans. I have pointed out and attempted to analyze only a few with case histories, isolated situations and illustrations. I now present my conclusions:

1. Some white females associate with and marry black males motivated by the female's natural desire and need of a man. The incidental fact of the man being black is not necessarily indicative of abnormality. A small percentage of white females associate with black males or marry them in areas where there is a lack of available white males.

2. Integration of the races in schools, industry, public recreational areas, dance halls, night-

clubs, and so on, have thrown the races together and is contributing to inter-race associations and marriage.

3. Integration will increase. Some white females are attracted to black males because of their skin color which contrasts the colorlessness of white skin.

4. Others are attracted to African-Americans' congenial and uninhibited personalities.

5. Many white females receive from the black male the attention and approval, they desire, which is not forthcoming from many white males.

6. Contrary to popular opinion, white women motivated by any of the aforementioned reasons can and do sincerely love their black males. The majority of women who are married to African-American males enjoy deeply warm, tender, and mutually satisfying relationships. They offer no apologies, have no regrets, and are agreed that if their present marriage failed or their husband died, they would seek another black mate.

7. Interestingly and significantly, a majority of the females that I interviewed manifested identifiable neurotic or abnormal characteristics or propensities, which are prevalent in American society.

Unfortunately this conclusion is supported and

reinforced by the numerous television talk shows: *Montel, Jennie Jones, Leeza, Rickie Lake,* and *Jerry Springer,* and especially the judge shows; *Judge Brown, Judge Judy, Judge Koch,* and *Judge Lane,* the most outrageous of them all which thankfully doesn't come on until around midnight.

These females, generally speaking, were insecure, unloved, or rejected or deserted by parents. Many come from unstable and dysfunctional home environments. Some were mentally and/or emotionally disturbed. Some sought relationships with black males out of rebellion and defiance. Still others as a means of escape from emotional hurt and pain.

CHAPTER 8
Mixed Blood Progeny

This chapter defines and clarifies misconceptions and myths concerning the progeny of white/black unions.

Nigger, Negro, Black, African-American: A person of the typical African branch of the black race; a black man; a person having more or less African blood. In the United States a person having one-sixteenth or more African ancestry.

Mulatto: The first generation offspring of a white person and an African. In popular use, any person of mixed Caucasian and African blood.

Quadroon: The offspring of a mulatto and a Caucasian; a person of quarter African ancestry.

Octoroon: The offspring of a quadroon and a Caucasian.

Mixed-Blood, Multi-Racial: A person of mixed Caucasian and African ancestry in varying degrees. In this treatise I will use these terms in preference with the exception

The contemporary black man, who is in many cases the product of amalgamation, is becoming increasingly lighter in complexion, and his hair texture is on a gradation from kinky to curly to naturally wavy to many cases straight. Facial features vary from Negroid with wide nostrils and large lips to aquiline nose and smaller lips. No longer can the black man be typically described as black in skin color with black kinky hair, beady black eyes, possessing fat lips and wide distended nostrils. It is impossible to distinguish all African-Americans on the basis of superficial physical characteristics of color and hair texture alone. Not too long ago two dignitaries from India were insultingly refused service from an upscale restaurant on the assumption that they were "Negroes." The restaurant was sued and lost the case.

It is safe to say that if present trends in integration, and birthrates in urban areas continue to escalate, along with a rising acceptance of interracial involvements, the complete amalgamation of the black man is not out of the realm of possibility. There are no reliable statistics but conceivably close to two million mixed-blood Americans have disappeared into the white race within the last twenty years, and this trend will increase. University of Wisconsin sociologist Robert Stuckert reported in a study that 21 percent of white Americans have some degree of African ethnicity. In this year of 1999 the percentage is even higher (Census Report, January 7, 1999).

Numerous persons who have spent time, energy, and

money tracing their family trees have been shocked and dismayed to find a black person resting in the branches of their ancestral tree.

Let us consider some pertinent questions. Do all progeny of interracial unions desire and attempt to pass for white? Do they resent their African ancestry? Are they emotionally disturbed because of having one white and one black parent?

We hear such cliches as, "I'm not opposed to interracial marriage, but I feel so sorry for the children. "Those poor little children will be rejected by whites and blacks alike." "All racially mixed kids are emotionally disturbed, that's why the crime rate is so high." "Interbreeding or crossbreeding of the races results in inferior offspring and eventual degeneration of the population."

Here's a myth that would be laughable if it were not believed by so many of the uninformed. "The half-breed transmits the bad qualities from both races to the offspring resulting in a definite mental and physical deterioration within the group, and may in some cases result in complete infertility." How ridiculous. There are undoubtedly evils attendant and attributable to race mixing, which are due to purely social, economic, and environmental factors, but there is not a shred of truth in the above statements. Such concepts have no basis in fact and are indicative of ignorance, stereotyping, and prejudice.

Identification with White Society

A small minority of mixed-bloods identify with white society. Usually these persons have a lighter skin color and curly or wavy brown hair and are not identified as African-American to the casual observer. In many instances they don't plan to pass, but are so assumed by white society. I, being of mixed ancestry, have been considered an American Indian, a man from India or Pakistan, even Egyptian.

On one occasion a cashier in a fast-food restaurant was very friendly. She asked if I was from Egypt like her. When I informed her that I was African-American, her demeanor changed immediately. She didn't say "thank you" when she gave me my order. I took it with a grain of salt. Perhaps after shortly coming to these shores she came under the influence of the American brand of racism, even though she was the same complexion as I am.

Many mixed-bloods escape the most blatant racism because of their complexions and facial beauty, finding doors of employment open. I don't know whether you have noticed the pleasing "coffee with cream" complexions of some television announcers and anchorpersons. Many who are third- and fourth-generation mixed-bloods with white skin and Caucasian features simply "pass" for white, sever all links to the past and have nothing to do with their black ancestors and family. They reveal no information about their relatives, saying that they all have died. Some claim to be orphaned or adopted. Some even change their names, securing new Social Security numbers and false identification papers. I wouldn't dare criticize or blame them because "survival" is the first law of nature.

Case in point: I'm multiracial. My grandmother who passed away in her middle nineties, Hattie, was the daughter of a slave master and one of his female chattels. After emancipation she met an ex-slave named James Gardner. They gave birth to James, Neely, Littleton our father, and Edgar. I've often wondered where in the world they came up with those names. They were the second generation. My father married our precious mother Lena, whose father was of almost a shocking blackness and whose mother was an American Indian. Both of our parents, who parented four boys and one sister, were brown complexioned with non-kinky hair. In fact, our mother's hair was straight black and shoulder-length. My brothers, now deceased, Littleton Jr., John, and Richard, all had brown eyes. I have hazel eyes and our dear sister Gertrude is lighter complexioned with grey eyes, taking after our grandmother. We are the third generation.

In 1946, at the age of twenty-two, I married a beautiful Caucasian, Katherine, of Scottish and English ancestry. Our three precious children; LeRoy Jr., Sharon, and Gordon are light complexioned with straight brown hair. Our daughter Sharon is highly successful in her profession and her ethnicity is of no concern. LeRoy Jr. married lovely Claudia, whose father was African-American and Indian and mother, Caucasian. Their two children have the same complexion as they have. Our son Gordon is a career serviceman stationed in Europe and married Marah, a beautiful English lady. They are the parents of a beautiful daughter, Maria, who is observably white in complexion. He is the fourth generation and dear Maria is the fifth. In our case it took five generations to obliterate observable African features.

If our granddaughter chooses to live as a Caucasian in a color-conscious world may God bless her because she certainly has mine.

As dear Maria matures she will undoubtedly have options to consider. If she were to ask me for my advice, I would list a number of what I would called "white privilege" advantages:

1. You will never be judged by the color of your skin, but by the content of your character....

   I recall the late Dr. Martin Luther King making reference to the problem in his historic "I have a dream" speech. He stated that one day in this great land of the free that his little children would not be judged by the color of their skin but by the content of their character. Sadly, that day had not dawned by the year of our Lord, 2000.

2. Whiteness will insure better job opportunities.

3. When you go shopping, you will not be put under surveillance by prejudiced security departments. And you will be courteously served.

4. When making purchases, your check or your credit card will be welcomed without question and without authentication.

5. You will not be embarrassingly detained and your carry-on bag will not be searched when boarding an airline flight.

6. If a police officer stops you, it will be for a legitimate traffic infraction and not because of your skin color. And you won't have to fear for your life or that illegal drugs will be planted in your automobile and then you will be searched.

7. You will not be discriminated against in a court of law.

8. You will not be discriminated against in renting housing or buying a home.

9. You will not be denied a bank loan nor a home mortgage, based solely on your skin color.

I could expand the list but the aforementioned will suffice.

I once officiated at the funeral of an elderly mixed-race gentleman who had been married to a white lady who preceded him in death. Their only daughter was observably white. The family lived in the black community and identified with its affairs, and attended a church that served the spiritual needs of black folk and social functions until the parents divorced. The mother and then adolescent daughter moved into the white community and severed all connection with the father's relatives and the black community. The daughter passed for white.

After reaching adulthood the daughter never married, feeling that her secret could best be kept by remaining single. She completed college, found employment in a large corporation, and rose to a position of responsibility. She lived a relatively secure but solitary existence. At the death of her father she inherited his sizable estate, which made her quite wealthy. She had wealth, but money doesn't fill the empty soul. She secured the services of an African-American mortician and myself in order to give her father, as she put it, a decent burial, yet conceal the fact of her African-American ancestry. There were no others in attendance; just her, the the funeral director, and myself.

I felt so sorry for her; in her hour of bereavement she bore her grief alone, uncomforted by friend or kinsman. After the committal service at the cemetery, she lingered before the open coffin weeping inconsolably and imploring her deceased father to forgive her; too late and too little. She, of course, was not guiltless, her mother bore the major responsibility for her isolated and lonely life by failing to instill in her daughter the moral values of truth and integrity.

One such boy grew up in our neighborhood, whose mother was impregnated by a white man he never knew. He had blond hair, blue eyes, and looked every bit white. He was an outstanding basketball player and very popular with the females, white and black. As an adult he found employment as a sales-man, married a white lady, moved out of the black community and proceeded to live and raise their two children as white. And why not? He certainly looked white, his wife was white, and his children were white, as designated on their birth certificates.

We who knew him did not resent him crossing the color-line or feel that he had abandoned his "people." For after all, in this race-oriented society, to be Negro or African-American is to look like it, and to be white is simply not to look Negroid.

Social scientists of questionable repute have theo-rized that mixed-race persons are an unhappy lot; re-jected by white and black societies alike, hence resent-ing their black ancestry.

The celebrated novel *Imitation of Life,* later pro-duced as a movie, fictionalized the case of a mixed-race female who resented and was ashamed of her African heritage. The plot was highly dramatic, but I felt that the dark-skinned mother was miscast which is of no con-sequence because the film starring Lana Turner was a box-office smash. Certainly there are such individuals, but they are not representative of the majority. I have known some who were disturbed because of their ancestry and others who were disturbed for other reasons. Decidedly, it would be unscientific and illogical to conclude, as some do, that all such are emotionally or mentally disturbed and are more mendacious, treacherous and dangerous than pure African-Americans.

The old wives' tale that one drop of black blood in a person can result in their offspring being completely black falls into the category of pure myth. Some persons, convinced that it is truth, cite personal knowledge of such occurrences in their hometown. According to the laws of genetics as researched and documented by the nineteenth-century scientist Gregor J. Mendel, it is scientifically and biologically impossible for two parents possessing an abundance of dominant genes of pigmentless skin and brown or blond or red hair to give birth to a black, woolly-haired baby.

When and if a dark-skinned infant is birthed, you can be assured that a "black lover" slipped in and out the back door. I unequivocally declare with documented scientific support, it takes more than one drop of black blood to produce a black baby.

Some mixed-bloods who pass for white believe this poppycock and refuse to produce offspring, fearing the possible birth of a black child.

Here is an amazing tale of one Reverend Benjamin...the illegitimate son of a white father and a mixed-race mother. He was passing for white, married and the pastor of a prominent church.

I was traveling and stopped in his suburb for a rest-stop and some breakfast. I noticed the church and, it being Sunday, decided to go in for the worship service. The church was well-filled with worshipers. I was impressed by the beauty of the sanctuary and was seated by a friendly usher. I noticed no other persons of color, which was not important.

After the service, the reverend greeted members of the congregation. When I approached and he shook my hand, he asked if I would remain a few minutes after as he would like to talk to me. I had thoroughly enjoyed the service and his sermon, and was in no hurry, so I gladly consented.

In the privacy of his study he confided that he had, as he put it, some Negro ancestry and felt that perhaps my presence was indicative of his secret being discovered. I assured him that this wasn't at all the case, which considerably relieved his anxiety.

We talked at length on a variety of subjects, including the so called "Negro problem," his ministry to an all-white congregation, and his plans for the future. Surprisingly, he seemed anxious to talk to a listening ear and so I lent him mine. Incidentally, a pastor who is a poor listener will not be successful; we must lend a sympathetic and nonjudgmental ear. I encouraged him to talk a little about his family and so the good pastor opened up. Although his mother had lavished attention and affection upon him, according to his testimony, he still blamed her for being promiscuous with a white man and spawning him. He was burdened as a child over his "bastard" status and despised his father for not publicly claiming him as a son.

His father had regularly visited his mother under cover of darkness, which deeply angered him because, as he stated, he knew full well what was going on in the bedroom. The father, who left early in the morning without even saying good-bye to him, would give the mother enough money each month to provide a modest living for them. His mother faithfully set aside a portion of the money for his education (which was indeed commendable).

Reverend Benjamin expressed, "Although I saw my father regularly, he never took me anyplace, not even to a ball game or a circus.

"The one thing he impressed upon me was even though I didn't look black, I was still one and shouldn't act uppity around whites. And above all don't mess around with white girls which can only get you in trouble."

Reverend Ben lamented, "Oh, how I longed to have a real father who would be there for me when I needed him."

I'll refer to him as Ben, not out of disrespect to his calling but in the context of the narrative. Ben's mother loved him dearly, but deeply harmed him by keeping him separated from his father.

The reverend's lifestyle was incompatible with his ministry. How can one preach the truth and live a lie?

Untruth flourishes in the darkness; truth survives only in the light. Falsity enslaves; truth redeems. Fidelity never induces bondage but bears the precious gift of freedom. The Bible teaches, "Ye shall know the truth and the truth shall make you free!"

Miss Miranda W....a mixed-race, white appearing, matronly type, never married and thought it cruel to bring children of African ancestry into the world, whose only "crime" is being born black. It is enigmatic that she didn't blame the racists, bigots, the perpetrators of racial hatred, prejudice, and discriminations for the plight of the black man in America but placed the blame at the feet of the victim.

Identifying with Black Society

There are condescending white persons who claim to have nothing against interracial marriage but feel sorry for the children of such unions.

An interracial couple answered an advertisement for an apartment for rent. The white landlady seemed quite disturbed while taking their application, expressing concern over what the other tenants might think about an interracial couple living on the premises. She required that they fill out a financial statement which would be presented to the credit bureau the next day and told them to call. She apparently couldn't contain herself any longer, reached over and patted their lovable olive-complexioned baby on its curly head and patronizingly said, "You poor, sweet little thing with one black parent and one white parent. It's a shame you can't be pure white."

The vast majority of mixed-race persons aren't plagued by a frustrating desire to be white and are perfectly satisfied to claim their African ethnicity and identify with their family and friends in the black community. Contrary to public opinion, they aren't ostracized by black persons for a number of reasons. First of all, a large percentage of African-Americans are amalgamated due to illicit and legitimate unions between the races. We feel kinship toward each other, therefore, it is unreasonable to conceive of amalgamated persons discriminating against their amalgamated families, kinsmen, and friends.

Further, because of the looser and less formal organization of the black family, the illegitimate issue of unions between white males or females and black males and white females are invariably accepted into the black family unit. Perhaps you're wondering; don't black folk have any moral standards? Of course we do, but under the amoral white-controlled socio-economic circumstances imposes upon us in America we have to often compromise for the sake of survival.

For instance, what would you do if you were being an African-American parent and your teenaged daughter was victimized and ravaged by a white male or males who were immune to prosecution? Your daughter, being afraid for her life or yours, would not dare give names or descriptions of her attackers. How would you go about finding the guilty? The police would give you no assistance and in some states even brutalize or arrest you for having the audacity to accuse white males. And then in some states at the beginning of the twenty-first century, it is no serious crime for a white man to beat or even kill a black person. In fact, in many instances white males feel that black females should consider it an honor to be sexualized by white males, regardless of consent.

One day while driving on a freeway overpass, I prevented a distraught young female from jumping down to the freeway in a suicide attempt. She was quite attractive, with a sepia complexioned face and a well formed body. I drove her over to the church, where we conversed. She needed someone to just talk to and I was a willing listener. She suffered from a sense of low self-esteem and worked as a prostitute, giving her earnings to a pimp.

She showed up for a few counseling sessions and even attended church on occasions. Despite my efforts she continued to practice her immoral professional of selling her "meat," as she expressed it, to Caucasian "johns" whom she despised.

One day at dawn, her lifeless, mutilated body was found in a wooded area. Little effort was made to solve the crime and shortly went on record as "unsolved."

What would you, being African-American, do if your precious wife came home with tears in her eyes and told you that her "boss" had forced himself on her and sexually violated her? Although incensed with rage, your better judgment would prevent you from seeking vengeance. Of course, there have been instances when vengeance was sought by an irate husband, who paid the consequences with a long jail sentence or his life.

Would you divorce your dear violated wife for adultery or infidelity? I think not. You probably would do what African-American males have done in this country for over a hundred years since emancipation: you would endure the circumstances, overlook the act, and continue to love your wife. You would treat her with sympathy and understanding and accept any children that would be born under such egregious circumstances. You would do your best to keep your family unit intact with love and commitment.

One African-American husband expressed this to me as I admired a darling baby in his arms, who was fair of skin with curly brown hair and hazel eyes, born to his brown-skinned wife and not fathered by him.

"I know the baby is not mine, but it was caught in my net. I love my wife and intend to stand by her. The baby needs a family, so I'll just be his father and love him along with the rest of my children: that's the least that I can do." I marveled at his selfless and compassionate solution to a highly difficult problem.

And of course, these mixed-blood children are very easy to love as they are, as rule, rather beautiful or handsome with attractive olive or brown complexions. In this color-conscious society, they strike a desirable medium between the sometimes stark blackness of the African and bland colorlessness of some white persons. Their hair has not the course kinkiness of the pure African or the too-straight limp-fine texture of the northern European. Their features tend to blend the facial features of the two races, usually making beautiful women and handsome men.

Many of them enjoy the advantageous psychological gratification of constantly having their physical attributes extolled. They are often the center of attention at social functions, which is certainly not conducive to emotional or mental disturbance. Males are often described as "dark and handsome" and the females as "exotic sepia beauties."

The majority of them experience few problems finding employment, since their appearance is no threat. I personally know many who appear to be of Italian, Greek, or Polynesian, or Arabian. I have been detained at the security checkpoint and had my carry-on bag was searched before boarding the plane on numerous occasions. I always inform the security personnel that I'm not an Arab, which probably doesn't allay their suspicion.

I recall that one college student was approached by a fellow student who inquired whether he was Greek or Italian, and was unsuccessful in convincing him that he had some African ancestry. He said that all through college, no one suspected that he was anything but Caucasian. He got along well with the professors and students alike. Notably, many Caucasians are uncomfortable only in the presence of persons who are observably of African ancestry

What follows is a most interesting notation brought to my attention and written by an intellectually brilliant educator/counselor of mixed-race ancestry who is not observably Negroid.

"I'm a male American of mixed-race ancestry who will not permit anyone to disavow my humanity. Some may not fully understand who I am, but I refuse to let them get away with disrespecting me. My father is of African ethnicity and my mother is Caucasian and I claim both. I refuse to permit anyone or any other culture to deny my status in this country or in the world. I refuse to let others define who I am and my sense of self-worth.

"Further, I will not, America, forget the infamy of the enslavement of persons of color on this continent. As long as there is a breath of life in my body, I will not forget. Thankfully, slavery is dead; segregation is moldering in the dust, but hope is alive. May we as Americans look to a brighter future of respect and inclusion for all people.

"The Bible challenges us to forgive and we shall be forgiven. Hence I declare emphatically, America, I forgive you but I will never forget!"

I certainly concurred with and applauded him. I have personally shaken off the dust of the past and look forward to the dawning of a new tomorrow.

CHAPTER 9
Dynamics of Amalgamation

The late Dr. Bell Wiley, former professor of history at Emory University during the 1960s in Atlanta, Georgia, was of the opinion that African-Americans are adolescent as a group and are in throes of growing and developing into a productive place in American society. He further contends that as the African-American gradually attains his goals of social, legal, and economic equality, he develops race pride, tends to integrate less and less with whites and is much less likely to intermarry with them. Surprisingly, there were many who concurred with his mythological conclusions.

Dr. Wiley failed to differentiate between illicit miscegenation, legitimate interracial marriage, integration, and social equality, and used them synonymously.

I disagree with Dr. Wiley's conclusions and will offer the following criticisms. First of all, I prefer not to use the term social equality, for it's a nonexistent state and never has and never will be an actuality in human relations. I personally dislike the term because it is hazy, nonfactual and in the minds of far too many conjures up visions of black males sitting in living rooms seducing white daughters or flitting in and out of white women's bedrooms. The term really defines nothing in actuality but erroneously implies only that which is negative.

Social association is in the province of personal preference and cannot be legislated. Individuals associate with individuals who suit their fancy and ignore those who don't.

The integration of public building and recreational facilities, licensed business establishments, and public conveyances, or buying a hamburger in a licensed restaurant catering to the public is not social equality. A black person going into a department store and being served in turn without deference to white patrons who come in after him is not social equality. The act of a black parent taking his children to a circus or a public zoo or purchasing a theater ticket and sitting in any available seat is not social equality. These activities are freedom pure and simple.

Please be advised, black Americans want freedom not an imaginary, elusive figment of some faulty thinker's imagination. And if anyone tells you anything different, don't you believe it.

The present developments in the race crisis facing America negate Dr. Wiley's contention that as the black American inches his way toward achieving his goals, he integrates less with whites.

The civil rights movement of the 1960s under the leadership of the late Dr. Martin Luther King had, among other goals, that of affecting integration in all areas not purely private. So, contrary to the opinions of the learned professor and others of his intellectual ilk, as we gain our goals we endeavor to integrate more, not less.

I would like to impress you with this consideration: integration is not synonymous with amalgamation. Since so many white racists and others fail to correctly differentiate between the two terms, I will clarify them.

America is a composite of many ethnic and racial minorities. All minority groups, except African-Americans, can live in their own communities and exercise social action within their own group, yet still be perfectly free to engage in social action in society at large. This is integration that embraces freedom. Integration, therefore, embraces the freedom of a group or individual to participate in the total life of American society without merging with the majority—minority identification is not lost. I hope this is making sense to you. In an integrated society, each minority group should ideally enjoy political, educational, social, vocational, economic, recreational, religious, and even marital freedom without recourse or losing its identity.

May we now define amalgamation: *Webster's New World Dictionary* defines "amalgamate": To unite, to combine into a whole, as two races, to mix making one…. In an amalgamated society, a minority group is completely absorbed by the majority group, losing its identity. This could conceivably happen in America over time by preventing the immigration of all ethnic groups except a continuum of Caucasian ethnics.

We shall now consider some of the dynamics of amalgamation as they pertain to African-Americans. From its inception, America has been a haven for the various ethnic groups comprising her populace. Oppressed people from all over the world, with the exception of the African, have come to her shores seeking freedom and opportunity. From the start, it was intended to exclude all peoples who were not of Caucasian ethnicity from the political process in this fair land. The American ideal as a democratic political system was founded upon the proposition or basis of a united humanity freely pursuing common goals. Immigrants representative of all races, except the black, were welcomed to these shores. So they came, the oppressed, the disenfranchised, the poor, the wretched masses yearning to be free. They came in teeming hordes seeking to turn dreams into reality, seeking a common destiny yet retaining their racial and national identity—English, Irish, Scandinavian, southern European; Italian, Greek, Spanish—yet Americans all.

To African-Americans, the words contained in the Declaration of Independence: "We hold these truths to be self-evident, that all men are created equal, that they are endowed by their Creator with certain unalienable Rights, that among these are Life, Liberty and the pursuit of Happiness," are a hollow mockery and are as "sounding brass and a tinkling cymbal."

With the introduction of the black to this continent, the ideal, the theory, remained, but the practice radically changed. Because of the extreme differences that characterized the black man, it was inconceivable that he could ever be assimilated into the mainstream of American society. The black man must ever remain a foreigner, an outcast, an alien in the land!

However, this was not destined, for in the more than three hundred years that have elapsed since the black man arrived, some highly significant changes have taken place on the American scene.

The strongest barrier to the social acceptance of African-Americans in this country is the widespread disapproval of interracial marriage, especially from southern white persons. This position is understandable considering the large concentration of black citizens in some areas, especially large metropolitan cities. There are at least 135 counties in nine southern states where black Americans outnumber white Americans. Since the voting rights legislation was passed during the tenure of the late President Lyndon Johnson, black voters have dramatically increased. As a result, black politicians are serving as mayors, judges, city council members, police chiefs and officers and educators. All this as been good for black citizens. A vote of thanks is certainly due to Rev. Jesse Jackson and his coalition to register voters. These gains have understandably caused alarm among white citizens in these areas.

These political gains have resulted in a broad spectrum of improvements in the lives of black citizens in the areas of economics, business development, job opportunities, and housing. Interestingly, the immigration of black Americans to the metropolitan cities of the North has slowed to a snail's pace. Literally thousands of African-Americans are moving south to take advantage of broadening opportunities.

The concern of many Caucasian Americans in the area is the impact of these developments upon interracial relationships.

In the year 1963, the United States Bureau of Vital Statistics recorded approximately 1,650,000 marriages; of this number there were perhaps 600,000 involving black persons. No firm statistics counted the number that were interracial. Author Robert Bell reported in his book *Marriage and Family Interaction* that about 2,000 interracial marriages occurred during that year, or approximately one in every 1,200 marriages or about 1.4 percent.

The reliability of these figures is questionable, based upon the 1990 census, which reported that more American citizens are marrying outside their racial groups. Inasmuch as this treatise is concerned only with white/black race mixing, I will confine my informational statistics to this context.

According to the latest Census Bureau findings,

more Americans are marrying outside their racial groups. The University of Michigan researchers compared the listing of black/white intermarriages in the 1950s of fewer than 2 percent to the 1992 Census data of 8 percent of black males between the ages of 24 to 35. The 1992 census data records 4 that percent of black females between the ages of 25 to 35 were interracially married.

In 1999, as I wrote this essay, new census data had not come out, but there is little doubt that the percentage of black/white relationships will continue to increase. In cities such as New York, Chicago, Detroit, Los Angeles, and Sacramento interracial marriages are at a ratio of about 2.2 percent. In the Twin Cities of St. Paul and Minneapolis, Minnesota which are noted for their liberal views on race relations, the ratio could easily exceed 2.9 percent. So it appears that is minimal chances of white female being courted by black swain; there is little cause for alarm.

Racial barriers are not as insurmountable as they appear, except in the minds of those who raise them. However, color prejudice is a social reality and must not be ignored or denied. No amount of idealistic rhetoric or legislation can make it disappear; only education, honest dialogue, and respect are the answers.

Young people considering an interracial relationship or marriage must recognize that it is unpopular and unaccepted in some circles. They must recognize that crossing the color line can create some serious problems, which must be met with mature judgment and wisdom.

The problems of employment and housing must be faced. They must exercise discretion in determining where they will live, what church they will attend, the friends they will associate with. There must be added to their love: strength of character, integrity, courage in the face of opposition, and the ability to stand together against the possible disapproval of family acquaintances and the social structure.

One astute thinking white gentleman said, "Interracial marriage is not an insoluble problem; it's a highly exciting and daily challenge." I heartily agreed with him.

At this juncture I can envision no immediate end to color-based prejudice nor a solution to the problem of interracial relationships or marriage between white and black Americans as long as chauvinistic racial pride, ignorance, and intolerance exist. Perhaps one day in the not too distant future there will dawn the daylight of tolerance and cooperation and reconciliation among the races, and respect for human rights and dignity will cover the nation as the waters cover the sea.

CHAPTER 10

Achievement

Judiciary

At the beginning of the twenty-first century the dream of the late Dr. Martin Luther King, Jr., charismatic civil rights leader, has not been fully realized, but it is still alive and we will not let it die.

- Great strides have been made in the arena of jurisprudence since pioneer lawyer John Swett Rock was admitted to the Massachusetts State Bar in 1861. This was indeed a landmark decision because the nation was embroiled in the Civil War and slavery was still legal. Attorney John M. Langston, graduate of Oberlin College in Ohio, was admitted to practice before the United States Supreme Court in 1867.

- In 1872, Charlette Ray became the first African-American woman admitted to the bar. Her pioneering led to a succession of females entering the law profession—Ms. Juanita Freeman, Patricia Roberts Harris, and Angela Davis, to name a few.

- In 1939 the-then mayor of New York City, Fiorello LaGuardia, appointed Jane Bolin as the first African-American female judge in the United States.
- In 1866, Constance Baker Motley was the first African-American woman to be appointed a federal judge in the southern district of New York.
- in 1921, Lena O. Smith was admitted to the bar in Minneapolis, Minnesota, whom I personally knew.

An increasing number of lawyers have been and are being admitted to the bar in the socially liberal state of Minnesota, where I was raised, educated, married, and with the support of my precious wife raised our children, and served in the pastorate for 40 years.

After the Civil War ended, numerous African-Americans migrated to Minnesota and, despite its inclement weather settled there.

- Attorney Frederick L. McGhee was admitted to the bar and opened a law office in 1889 in the capital city of St. Paul, Minnesota.
- John F. Wheaton, a pioneer graduate of the University of Minnesota in 1894, opened his law office in Edina, a mostly white suburb of Minneapolis. He was elected to the state legislature.

- I was interested to learn that in 1898, Charles W. Scrutchin opened his law office in Bemidji, Minnesota, which is almost to the Canadian border. His clientele had to have been Caucasian. Perhaps brother Scrutchin embraced the position of an elderly Minnesotan who stated to me, "It's easier to struggle in a snowstorm than it is to escape from the Ku Klux Klan."

- In 1901, McCants Stewart was the first African-American to receive a master of law degree from the University of Minnesota.

- Attorney Macio Littlejohn was elected justice of the peace in Walker, Minnesota, in 1941. A few years later, he relocated to St. Paul and I had the good pleasure of meeting him.

I once sued a defendant in the Ramsey County Municipal Court. Attorney M….represented him. Not being an attorney, I appeared "pro se." I must say, Perry Mason could not have presented a more brilliant case. I won.

As we left the courtroom, I overheard the defendant berating Attorney M… "You sure didn't earn your damn fee. My money went down the drain!"

The defendant spied me and extended his hand as he approached.

"If I ever need a lawyer again, I'll call you."

I smilingly answered, "Sorry, I'm not a lawyer, I'm just a humble preacher." Interestingly, we later became friends and he made an investment in one of my projects.

- Before Attorney James Bradford became special assistant attorney general in 1955, I hired him for a case involving a writ of *habeas corpus*. I was released from custody and didn't even have to appear before the judge. Bradford performed excellently. He was an outstanding choice for special assistant attorney general.

- I was also pleased when my friend Attorney Stephen L. Maxwell was appointed Assistant Ramsey County Attorney in 1959. In 1967 he was appointed judge of the Ramsey County District Court. The "folks" rejoiced; we now had a friend in the court!

- Attorney William Posten. A personal friend appointed Assistant Hennepin County Attorney in 1961 and in 1973 was appointed judge of the Hennepin County Municipal Court. In 1976 he was elevated to judge of the Hennepin District Court.

- In 1978, Attorney Charles H. Williams, Jr. was appointed Ramsey Public Defender. He may have been the youngest appointee, or perhaps he just looked young. I personally knew the family through his father, Dr. Charles Williams who was my dentist. The black community was indeed diminished when Dr. Williams passed away. We needed him, as many white dentists refused service to persons of color.

As public defender, Charles Williams, Jr. was very effective, providing legal service to many impoverished African-Americans. His competence was noticed, and in 1988 he was appointed referee of the Ramsey County District Court.

- In 1982, Attorney Donald Lewis was appointed U.S. attorney district of Minnesota. I have fond memories of him, as we talked on occasions. He served with distinction.

- Attorney Pamela Alexander was appointed judge of the Hennepin County Municipal Court in 1983, becoming the first African-American woman to be so honored. I was gratified because I remember coaching her father Robert Bellison on a basketball team at the Ober Boys Club, St. Paul, in 1945. The adage is "time marches on" but the reality is "time rushes on." Tall Pamela, taking her height from her dad, has now become a judge: what a pleasant consideration.

There were and are others who have distinguished themselves in the legal arena in the State of Minnesota.

Slavery was legalized, and was abolished by the 13th Amendment to the Constitution. It was legalized by law, and abolished by law.

AMENDMENT XIII

Section 1
Abolition of Slavery

Neither slavery nor involuntary servitude, except by punishment for crime whereof the party shall have been duly convicted, shall exist within the United States, or any place subject to their jurisdiction.

AMENDMENT XV

Section 1
Negro Suffrage

The right of citizens of the United States to vote shall not be denied or abridged by the United States or by any State on account of race, color, or previous condition of servitude.

The law is now on our side and it was decided to take full advantage of the law. African-American lawyers have done more to advance the struggle for justice and self-determination for persons of color than any other profession. It is only in the courts that justice can finally be meted out.

- Some may have called it fate, or destiny, or divine intervention, or maybe all of them combined when attorney Thurgood Marshall appeared in the law arena 1935. In that year he and Attorney Charles Hamilton, representing the NAACP, won a landmark decision for black students to the University of Maryland. In 1950 he was appointed director-counsel of the NAACP Legal Defense Fund. His competency in law was recognized when he was appointed to the federal bench as a circuit judge in 1961.

History was made in 1967 when President Lyndon B. Johnson nominated Attorney Marshall to the Supreme Court, making him the first African-American Supreme Court justice. Controversial Clarence Thomas is the second African-American to serve on the Supreme Court.

The battle continues because racism, race based indignities, and discrimination are still practiced on virtually every level of the court system. We are grateful for the myriad of judges and magistrates who operate from a moral and legal basis and mete out justice. Hope is alive and we will not let it be denied.

Politics

By taking advantage of the ballot, African-Americans are turning the tide in the political arena. Across America there are mayors of color in many major cities. African-Americans are serving on city councils and commissions, as court officials, and police chiefs.

- Ronald H. Brown, a distinguished attorney, was elected chairman of the Democratic National Committee on February 10, 1989. He was the first African-American to be elected head of a major national political party. The nation was saddened when he was killed along with all passengers and personnel in an airplane crash on April 3, 1996. Hope is alive! Vote, baby, vote!

Increasing numbers of black senators and representatives are being elected to Congress.

- In 1870, former slave Hiram R. Revels, a Republican legislator from Mississippi, became the first African-American senator in Congress. He served from February 25, 1870 to March 3, 1871.

After Reconstruction and the enactment of the poll tax, the enfranchisement of black Americans came to a standstill.

When voting rights were reinstated blacks literally rushed to the polls, and we have not relented and will not because we realize that the vote is one of the most effective weapons in our quest for self-determination.

- Texas-born dynamic orator Barbara Jordan was the first African-American elected to the state senate in 1966. She made history when in 1972 she was the first black and the first black woman elected to Congress from Texas. The nation lost an icon when she died in 1996.

- Shirley Chisholm, a dynamic activist was elected to Congress in 1968, becoming the first African-American congressperson. I was greatly impressed with her political savvy until she launched a presidential campaign. What in the world was she thinking of: her chances of success were totally nil. However, she was not the first or the last to harbor a misconception of their dubious popularity and succeed only in enhancing others' financial status.

- Carol Moseley-Braun was elected as a first to Congress during President William Clinton's reign and championed the fight to pass the President's $22 billion plan to build and refurbish and modernize schools nationwide.

- Detroit native Charles C. Diggs, a Michigan

Democrat, was elected to Congress in 1954 and distinguished himself during 25 years of service. He retired in 1979 and died in 1988.

- Democratic congressman from Georgia who was involved as a civil rights activist with Dr. Martin Luther King, Jr. during the 1960s and continues to fight for justice and self-determination for all citizens.

- Democratic representative from Michigan Charles Rangel.

- Congressman Jesse L. Jackson, Jr., son of the renowned activist Rev. Jesse L. Jackson.

Medical Profession

- Great strides have been made in the medical profession since Dr. Daniel Hale Williams successfully performed the first open-heart surgery in 1893. Born in 1856 in Hollidaysburg, Pennsylvania, he earned his medical degree from Chicago Medical College in 1883. He established Provident Hospital, an interracial facility that afforded the Black community medical services.

- Dr. Charles Drew gained international acclaim when he isolated blood plasma. He was involved in an automobile crash and denied medical aid at "white only" local hospitals, causing his tragic and premature death. The world was denied his genius because of the curse of racism. African-American physicians continue to make progress in all fields, including dentistry. Hope is still alive!

Highly skilled brain surgeon Dr. Benn Carson gained worldwide acclaim when he successfully separated Siamese twins who were joined at the skull. He is a director of pediatric neurosurgery at John Hopkins Hospital in Baltimore, Maryland. He has coauthored a first book, *Gifted Hands,* with Cecil Murphy and a second with Gregg Lewis entitled *The Big Picture* (Zondervan).

The medical profession desperately needs physicians of color in order to level the field in view of the fact that persons of color, not just African-Americans but Orientals, Asians, Latinos, Arabs, Indians (Native American and immigrants), and Polynesians are still victims of "color discrimination" in the medical service arena. Medical studies have established that persons of color receive inferior services and care as opposed to Caucasian patients.

During slavery, medical treatment was denied ill and ailing slaves. Treatment if any was provided by witch doctors who were not trained in medical sciences, but instead used herbs and lotions coupled with superstitions. Epidemics often wiped out all of the chattels on a plantation who were ill, endangering the ones who were not and even members of the slave master's family. The weak perished and the strong survived.

After emancipation, as slaves migrated to other states and areas, health services for blacks were minimal or unavailable. Hospitals as a rule, especially in the South, denied persons of color admittance. The hospitals in the North that did provide admittance to persons of color were highly suspect.

The infamous Tuskegee experiment was merely the tip of the iceberg: 500 black males were paid a stipend to participate in an experiment to find a cure for the common cold. Under this guise they were inoculated with syphilis bacterium. Amazingly, some kicked the infection and lived to a ripe old age.

I had the privilege of meeting one of these test subjects in Minneapolis in the middle 1960s. He suffered with arthritis, had lost all of his teeth, and his legs were horribly scarred, but he was unimpaired mentally. The saying was, "First they try it on a guinea pig, then on a god, next on a monkey, and finally on a big 'buck' black man."

In St. Paul, Minnesota, where our family moved to in 1925, there was the St. Joseph's Hospital under the jurisdiction of the Catholic Diocese of St. Paul which provided services to all persons.

The Wilder Dispensary (not a hospital, but a clinic)

was funded by the Wilder Foundation and served all persons regardless of ethnicity. Our dear mother was diagnosed with tuberculosis there, and medical examinations and pharmaceuticals were provided for our family. Tubercles were found in my lungs, which later calcified. I recall no hospitalization, so God must have touched me because He is still using me to preach the Gospel in my seventy-fifth year. Pop singer James Brown coined the phrase, "I feel good!" So I join in.

We realize that during the Depression years of the 1930s medical science was in its infancy; no cures for tuberculosis, infantile paralysis (polio), chicken pox, scarlet fever, meningitis, whooping cough, and numerous other diseases and ailments. We knew little about services for white people at Anker Hospital, but an alarming number of black patients were released as corpses; including my dear mother, who died of tuberculosis, and my father who died of cancer in both lungs. I'm so glad the unethical practices and outright lies of the tobacco industry have been exposed. I along with many others would be very pleased, in fact, overjoyed, if production, distribution, and sale of tobacco products were declared illegal.

The notorious Anker Hospital provided services to all citizens, but was under suspicion by us. The black community was alarmed at the number of females sterilized there after birthing a child born out of wedlock. If they did not consent, their names were removed from the welfare rolls. I knew of one teenage male who was castrated under suspicious circumstances, and young Cody, who died during brain surgery.

I remember Carl Kubiac, a white boy who lived across the street from us, who survived polio with a shortened and stiff leg and had to walk with a limp and a cane. I was not fearful of playing with him as many our age were.

I cite my own nightmarish experience at Dr. Frankenstein's Castle. About 1933, I along with a number of black youth whose families were on welfare were taken from the rooms of McKinley Elementary School to Anker Hospital. Without our parents' consent our adenoids and tonsils were surgically removed. Of course, it was not revealed that we were guinea pigs for interning surgical students. My father was furious, came to the hospital, picked me up in his arms, and carried me out to a taxicab. I bled all night long and could have perished. God was with me; I recovered. We rejoiced when Anker was torn down during World War II.

During the Depression years we had two African-American doctors and one dentist in St. Paul: Dr. Brown and Dr. Cump, who came to our homes, and the dentist Dr. Butler, who set up his practice in his basement. After World War II, Dr. Charles Williams started his practice in a commercial building in a so-called white neighborhood, serving all citizens. Apparently his level of skill was so excellent, his ethnicity was overlooked by his white clientele. In fact, he was elected president of the St. Paul Dental Association. Just in passing, in 1953 he put a gold bridge in my mouth and assured me that it would last at least twenty-five years: it's still service-able forty-six years later. The city lost a valued servant when he passed away, because most white dentists re-fused to serve persons of color.

The unpleasant reality is, at the end of the twentieth century, color discrimination still persists. A study funded by President William Clinton's administration showed that many physicians provide different levels of treatment and service based upon the patient's race, gen-der and the economic status. It was discovered that black patients are more likely to die from heart disease than Caucasians. Similar differences hold true for cancer patients.

Research reported in the *New England Journal of Medicine* suggests that black patients with congestive heart problems have a higher risk of death. Researchers at the National Heart, Lung and Blood Institute found that 42 percent of African-American patients treated for congestive heart condition died compared with 36 per-cent of Caucasian patients.

Previous studies concluded, higher death rates for African-Americans from heart disease may be due to hormonal differences. Hogwash!

Education

I applaud the increasing number of high school administrators, principalss and teachers.

"A mind is a terrible thing to waste." This theme of the United Negro College Fund, which was suggested by the distinguished lawyer Vernon Jordan, could be better rendered, "A mind is too valuable to waste." So be it, I sincerely embrace the agenda that is dedicated to serving the educational needs and opportunities of African-American youths.

The 1998 report issued by the Southern Education Foundation, located in Atlanta, Georgia, caused grave concern. The report entitled "Miles to Go" focuses on 18 southern states that once practiced segregation in institutions of higher learning. The states featured in the report are Alabama, Arkansas, Delaware, Florida, Georgia, Louisiana, Maryland, Mississippi, Missouri, North Carolina, Ohio, Oklahoma, Pennsylvania, South Carolina, Tennessee, Texas, Virginia, and West Virginia.

The study documented minimal increases in the number of African-American faculty members within the last 30 years. The number of African-American students has increased less than 2 percent during that period and a dismally low number have graduated. Despite these developments, we must not let our hope die.

The late Dr. Martin Luther King's dream of little

black children and little white children sitting together and learning together in unsegregated classrooms must include students of all ethnicities learning together in college classrooms.

Recognition must be given to leaders who have paved the way, such as Mary McCleod Bethune (1875-1955) founder of Bethune-Cookman College and the National Council of Negro Women; Booker T. Washington, Tuskegee Institute; Johnetta Betsch Cole, the first black woman to become the president of Spelman College; Marva Collins, founder of Marva Collins Preparatory School; California college professor and activitist Angela Davis; Dr. David Taylor, dean of the General College, University of Minnesota. The list could go on and on, but I will let those whom I have named suffice. The dream is becoming a reality and hope will not be denied!

I concur with the views of the distinguished former pastor and founder of the OIC program, Dr. Leon Sullivan who stated, "Education opens the doors to jobs, vocational opportunities, and success in other fields." I was greatly impressed with his best selling book of yesteryear, *Learn, Baby, Learn,* I hope it is still in libraries across the nation.

Business

African-Americans have made significant inroads in the fields of industry and business: manufacturing, distribution, auto dealerships, fast-food franchises, real estate brokerages, and insurance.

In the field of finance, black owned banks, mortgage companies, finance companies, and stock brokerages are on the increase. In the last thirty years there have been increasing business successess, and there is every indication that will continue. Millions of African-Americans have come to the realization that the road to financial success and security is to have something to sell other than entertainment and athletic ability.

I join Rev. Jesse Jackson, Dr. Leon Sullivan, financial genius John Rogers, Jr. of Chicago-based Areil Capital Management, stock brokerage, and others who have challenged; "grow it; produce it; cook it; manufacture it; package it; advertise it; market it."

We African-Americans have been consumers far too long. It is now time for us to become producers and marketers. We need to note the example of the Jewish immigrants, who came from Europe at the turn of the century, congregated in areas, and opened businesses to serve the needs of the community. When I was growing up we used to say, "What ever you need, a Jew is selling it." And the blessing for us was that they would hire us. They owned a variety of businesses: the ma and pa grocery, the meat market, the fish store, the tailor shop and the dry cleaners. I worked for a number of dry cleaning establishments before I was called into the Christian ministry. I finally saved enough money to open my own store. I rented space in a shoe repair business from elderly Mr. Anderson. I purchased a steam boiler, a presser, a Susie-Q, and a steam iron for finishing shirts, a cash register, and I was in business. I got the garments dry cleaned by the pound at wholesale and finished them at my store. I was so grateful for the support and assistance from the Jewish dry cleaners. I expressed one day to one of them who responded, "I appreciate your thanks, but the reality is that we need you people as much as you need us because you people catch most of the hell here in America, which gives us a chance to survive. There were none of you people in Germany, so we caught it all."

We shook hands and I departed his establishment. I pondered his words and kept them in my soul. I felt a kindredship with him, for anti-Semitism is as deadly a curse as white racism. May God have mercy on us.

We should note the business activities of the Orientals, Asians, and immigrants from Pakistan and India. They are not waiting in line at the Welfare Department, hoping to receive assistance. They are not making out an application for a job; they make their own jobs.

I applaud the many who have risen to the pinnacle of financial success. I list some of these who have attained the status of leaders, mentors, and fine examples:

- John H. Johnson and wife Eunice, founder of the Johnson Publishing Company in 1942, which also publishes *Jet* magazine and markets books authored by black writers.

- 87-year-old Edward Davis, the first African-American to own an auto dealership. Black business-persons now own dealerships in most major cities across America.

- Astute Pamela Rodgers, owner of a Chevrolet dealership who has demonstrated that we are capable of more than being just office workers and can successfully operate on the highest level.

- Former NFL star Mel Farr, who operates the largest chain of black-owned auto dealerships in the Detroit area, comprised of 15 dealerships that provide jobs for literally hundreds of African-Americans.

- Bill Cosby, inimitable comedian and entrepreneur. He along with his wife are generous contributors to numerous charities and programs.

- Late Chicago Bears football great and NFL Hall of Fame inductee, Walter Payton, a founding Director of First Northwest Bank in Arlington, Heights, Illinois, and owner of Walter Payton Power Equipment Company.

- Oprah Winfrey, owner of her own production company, which produces the top-rated Oprah Winfrey television show and numerous movies. She is a nationally known star, entrepreneur, and philanthropist.

- Former Lakers star, Earvin "Magic" Johnson's real estate company develops real estate projects and owns a multiplex theater complex in Los Angeles, California.

- Malcolm Jamal-Warner, actor, producer, entrepreneur.

- Earl Graves, entrepreneur and publisher of *Black Enterprise* magazine.

- Isiah Thomas, former NBA star and part owner of the Toronto Raptors NBA franchise. He recommends that high salaried athletes invest heavily in business enterprises because the day will surely come when their talent and popularity will wane and their services will not be marketable.

- I wholeheartedly endorse Rev. Jesse Jackson's commitment to the goals of the PUSH Coalition and its initiative to encourage black Americans to invest in business enterprises and stocks and bonds. He declares that the "new chains of slavery are credit cards and lottery tickets." I add visiting casinos in the dead hope of winning a fortune. The sure winners are the Native American tribes that own and operate the casinos. Invest, baby, invest!

The war over racism in America still rages. And we as a people will continue to fight with the song, "We shall overcome," on many fronts. We will not relent; we will not retreat. We survived slavery. We overcame segregation and the Depression of the 1930s. We as Americans of African ethnicity will overcome and one day in the not too distant future claim VICTORY! Hope is still alive and we will not let it be denied.

I dared not dream that in my lifetime there would appear on the political a scene an African-American who would capture the hearts of Americans from all walks of life. Following his outstanding generalship in Operation Desert Storm, President William Clinton appointed him chairman of the Joint Chiefs of Staff of the United States Armed Forces. After serving briefly, Colin Powell retired. He was touted as a likely candidate for the presidency of the United States which he declined. Based upon poll counts, I feel that he would have been elected by a wide margin, and become the first African-American President. The course of history would have been changed!

I contend that even though he would have been the first, he wouldn't have been the last. My prediction is that in the not too distant future, an African-American will be elected to the highest office in the land. He or she will be from the fifth, possibly sixth, generation of their family tree and will be nearly white in complexion. I'm certain the candidate will not be the complexion of Supreme Court Justice Clarence Thomas.

CHAPTER 11
Prognosis

I predict that if the present trend of race mixing continues in America for the next six to eight generations, there will be no citizens with observable African/Negroid features. A biological evolutionary phenomenon is operating which started during slavery, when the first slave owner impregnated one of his female slaves. The mixed-race offspring resulting from this relationship often got involved sexually with white persons, and because of their complexion they were in great demand as "house" servants. In cases of incest, the "quadroon" offspring were highly prized on the slave market. Such females were used as breeders and low-paid prostitutes.

During the twenty or so generations of slavery and segregation in the southern states, literally, millions of white and black persons unknowingly contributed to the biological process of genetic selection for the survival of the species. In view of the fact that the African is not genetically programmed for survival in the northern hemisphere, his eventual demise in America is inevitable.

On the other side of the equation, which is baffling, some Europeans, males and females, are inexplicably attracted to African-Americans, which perpetuates the phenomenon. It takes five to eight generations for the offspring to become genetically Caucasian. In fact, there are literally millions of Caucasians who have no knowledge of some African ethnicity in their roots.

The white Supremacists who espouse that race mixing will result in the mongrelization of the white race are scientifically in error. Instead it will result in the eventual demise of the black race.

The following developments contribute to this trend:

- The moral decline in America. Promiscuous and premarital sex is widely practiced.

- The television and motion picture industries are lifting barriers. No longer is interracial romancing, kissing and simulated sexual activity taboo.

- The secular music and entertainment industries feature love/sex and adultery across racial lines.

- The ACLU champions the First Amendment, right to engage in sex with whomever and wherever one chooses.

- The federal government:

  Antimiscegenation laws have been removed from the Constitution.

  Interracial marriage is now legal in all states.

  Immigration laws favor Europeans; thousands are admitted daily.

Quotas for Africans are lowering, and I predict will become even more restrictive.

- Society:

  An article published in the September/October 1999 issue of the *Vital Ministry Magazine* states that according to the *U.S. Census Bureau's Report*, whites will be a minority by 2050, and today's minorities combined will be a majority. According to census demographer Robert Perkins, at present the biggest immigration groups are Hispanics and Asian-Pacific Islanders.

I contend that the Census Bureau's calculations are seriously flawed. Census Bureau Director Kenneth Prewitt admits that Census 2000 needs to be more complete and accurate.

By 2050, if present trends continue, my opinion is that there will be an increase in the number of Hispanics, Asians, Orientals, and African-Americans getting involved sexually and intermarrying with Caucasians. The population will reflect an increasing percentage of Americans of Caucasian ethnicity. If the world continues until the year 3000, Americans of Caucasian ethnicity will be the majority. Perhaps then America will finally become the land of the "FREE."

TABLE 1

Race of Wife by Race of Husband: 1960, 1970, 1980, 1991, and 1992 (5k)

U.S. Census Bureau

Source Of Data

The tabulations show data from the 1990, 1980, and 1970 censuses. The 1990 tabulations source is the 5-percent Public Use Microdata Sample (PUMS). The 1980 data for the Total, White, and Black populations are from the 1980 5-percent PUMS and those from the 1970 census are based on the 20-percent sample.

The data on married couples are based on information reported in the decennial census, not marriage certificates. The children are the householder's own, step, or adopted children, as reported in the census. The householder is the person in whose name the housing unit is owned or being rented.

The number of children in mixed-race households was obtained by cross-tabulating the race of the child by the race of the mother and father in married-couple households for the four major race groups (White, Black, American Indian, Eskimo, and Aleut; and Asian and Pacific Islander). Children under 18 years of age in married-couple families were identified as residing in a mixed-race household if the race for the parents, stepparent, or unmarried partner and child living in the household are different, or if the race reported on the census form for the child differs from that of at least one parent, stepparent, or unmarried partner.

All data are subject to sampling variability, respondent classification errors, and data processing mistakes. The Census Bureau has taken steps to minimize errors. However, because of methodological differences use caution when comparing these data with data from other sources.

Table 1

TABLE 1

Numbers in Thousands	1992 Current Population Survey	Percent Distribution
Interracial couples 3/	1,161	2.2
Black / White	246	21.2
Black husband/White wife	163	66.3
White husband/Black wife	83	33.7

(See pages 152ff. for discussion)

For Further Information

Contact: Racial Statistics Branch, U.S. Census Bureau, (301) 457-2402.

GLOSSARY

Amalgamation: The biological or genetic union of pesons of different races.

Ethnic: A minority group having common customs, language and social views, etc.

Ethnicity: Ethnic classification or affiliation.

Genotype: Genes transmitted from parents to offspring.

Hegemony: Influence or authority of one nation or group of people over others.

Interrracial marriage: Marriage between persons of different races.

Miscegenation: Racial intermixture

Mongrel: Derogatory reference to a mixed race person.

Mulatto: A person of white and black racial ethnicity

Race: A grouping of people having similar physical characteristics.